Healing

Through Light

Awareness

By Lucy Devine

978-1-915502-47-6

Orla Kelly Publishing
27 Kilbrody,
Mount Oval,
Rochestown,
Cork,
Ireland.

Index

I wish to dedicate this book to my parents.

Lucy Devine works as a healer, and facilitates Light that helps people heal and meditate, which will, in time, build as their personal awareness. She spent over twenty years training to be a healer and continues to live each day enhancing her awareness to ensure she is a better healer.

Her books are a source of information on how to begin to heal and meditate, providing meaningful insights and new skills that enhance people's lives.

She offers the following:

- Individual and group healing sessions
- Individual meditation and group meditation session
- Dream interpretation
- Readings that provide insight and clarity
- Cutting of the ties sessions.

She is a registered healer with the National Trust. Healer number H22229.

Note from Author

Healing Through Light Awareness is my book about meditation and self-healing. I have written it with truth, hoping it inspires you through meditation, with insight and prayers to articulate your pain and distress.

This book is the third in a trilogy about healing and self-healing.

It provides the tools that will enable you to unravel your mind. Also, it will encourage you to seek your Light within, to build and maintain your unique connection with Light. By seeking the Light within, you build awareness of your higher self, which reveals how your mind works.

All my books reflect the journey I revealed to myself as I turned my senses inward to find my darkness, the mental and spiritual pain in my mind, and how I connected to my Light within that began my self-healing journey.

These books do not tell you how to gain power over people by telling them what to do or how to imitate others; instead, they empower you to think with Light awareness. Neither do these books give the reader false hope when I tell you I have seen how Light lifts pain by miraculous means.

I found and connected to Light in my meditation. I found my courage through my prayers. I found my truth by accepting the existence of the Light within me. The truth of my interpreted Light became my default as it shone and continues to brighten my learned reality, which is my mind. I protect my higher self-awareness by applying my Light boundaries, which enable me to build my Light awareness as the challenges on this journey were, at times, harrowing.

There is no magic cure to heal the pain and the darkness of the mind, but if people do not try to recognise and release their mindsets, the pain of the mind will manifest in the body in the shape of the diseases we all dread.

This book will help build self-awareness by inspiring you to ask questions about yourself, your thinking, your beliefs, your education, your family dynamic and society in general. In my experience, the self-healing journey begins by asking, who is God.

How I Healed my Mind is the title of my second book. This book revealed how the journey of darkness in my mind began for me, reflecting how the journey begins for each human being. It happens the instant the endocrine systems of the unborn baby and its mother activate to release their adrenaline into and around the unborn baby in the womb to help the baby be born. The birth journey facilitates the baby's mind to awaken into its unique existence. The baby's mind awakens to a sense of power. The powerful surges of hormonal power are automatically accepted to be the mind's entitled natural unique power. As the baby grows, the mind begins its unknown and automatic quest to own this power. Initially, the baby's mind searches and looks outwards toward the mother for power.

The baby is satisfied in its quest for power through the mother's nurturing as it learns to accept her ways, her thinking and her responses as the baby's truth. The baby learns to suppress its unique integral truth of self and automatically accepts the mother's truth and the family dynamic as its truth, which is an extension of the mother's mindset.

The senses of each individual always vibrate in the truth of Light. But unfortunately for humanity, the mind automatically suppresses the truth of Light because it senses it as weak, vulnerable, and not strong. Yet, the mind continues to search for the elusive powerful feelings it felt when it awakened during the birth journey.

The endless quest develops into a complex existence of survival and pain by the mind. The automatic suppression of personal feelings creates and builds the emotions of rejection, abandonment, loneliness, and isolation for the human mind. These unknown, hidden emotions, along with the invisible influences of shadowed spirits, create the energy that fuel depression, bipolar, anxiety, addiction, and all the other diseases within the mind. They are all self-created and are generated on a second-by-second basis by a person's mental perspective.

My Invisible World is the title of my first book. I began to write this book when I started my career in spiritual healing. At the time, I wanted to become the best spiritual healer I could be. The book reveals how I discovered my senses and how they work, the invisible world of my aura, my chakras and how they work. I discovered how and where my feelings come from and how emotions form. I discovered the control of the mind.

I found my mental and spiritual hidden and unknown pain. I reveal how I was diminished in how I saw myself and in my knowledge of myself through my schooling and my family's learned thinking dynamic. I discovered the Light within my heart chakra. From the truth of my Light within, I revealed how I was trying to become a spiritual healer through my learned spiritual and religious learning, which were fuelling my internal darkness. This negative learning revealed how I was coping as a wife and mother.

When you read these books from your perspective of self-questioning, you will find Light, and Light will help you heal.

Light can help you change your life by empowering you to make new choices.

Who is God?

I discovered that God is not a man, nor is He the external identity I learned to look up to and adore. God is not the judging damning force that casts souls away to hell or purgatory. God is not in the shape of a father's image to save me and keep me in my child's mind in heaven.

The following is my awareness of who God is.

I believe through my Light awareness that God is a nucleus of very subtle sensory sensations of the highest Light within the universe and my heart chakra. I have learned that I need to attune to this nucleus of Light reality one sense at a time. It has also been my experience that when I do not grow into each sensation's awareness, I cannot experience the Light's higher sensations. Therefore, my interpretations of Light are subtle feelings of wholeness within me and in my awareness.

These insights are a staggering internal growth for me as for most of my life my mind was a conflicted, painful mindset of a person I did not want to be. Is this growth not genuinely empowering? Of course, the only person who can see this miracle within me is me. The only person stopping me from gaining greater insight into God is my mind and my learned conditioned thoughts about myself and society.

The only force of energy that is damning and forthright is within my bravado mind reality.

As I grow in my acceptance of God's sensations within me, I recognise these sensations as the unconditional love that is God.

The revelation of unconditional love into my awareness has revealed my automatic desire to seek and feel conditional love and my desperate want to be loved conditionally.

I began my acceptance of unconditional love within me by sharing it with my children. Then, I began to express it through my Light boundaries; this was my first experience communicating and sharing unconditional love.

The crazy thing about this statement is that we all think we know how to love. It is the only thing most of us are confident of, and it is the thought process of assuming love that derails the mind into a delusion and illusion of what love is.

This ideology of conditional love instantly fuels the automatically entitled assumption about God, God's power, God's suffering, and God's purpose.

As I grew up, the only time I heard about love was in our religion classes when we heard how to love through the example of pain and sacrifice shown to us by God and his son, Jesus.

The Light Within

What is Light?

I heard very simply during my meditation that Light is the opposite of darkness.

Light and darkness exist within us all.

I call the Light within my heart chakra my higher self.

My darkness, I call my mind.

I accept that most people know that there is a sacredness within us.

Religions tell us this sacredness is our soul.

I believe this sacredness is Light.

Light is the unknown, invisible thread of God within humanity that knits us together in the higher vibrations of the Light that I call God.

Light frequencies vibrate in peace, joy, beauty, calmness, and tranquillity. Light frequencies are my intuited wisdom of God, which I call Light awareness.

Light frequencies are what I aim to evolve in each conscious moment of my living.

Light awareness is neither power-based nor powerlessness induced.

It is neither male nor female.

Instead, it radiates the wholeness of unconditional love, which is all-encompassing within each human being.

I discovered I could not bargain with Light, I could not manipulate it, and I could not control it. Therefore, I could not learn about Light.

I needed to sense and interpret Light. However, I could not teach the awareness of Light or help people learn about Light's meaning which caused frustration in people trying to find Light. Most people know how to learn and absorb knowledge, and they are reluctant to let go of this learning technique that has made them successful people. However, letting go of this learning technique becomes a significant barrier when someone is trying to attune to their senses.

I learned I can only inform and share information about Light. It is up to each person to decide to seek their Light for themselves. Each person decides for themselves when to begin to accept the existence of their Light within their heart chakra. A person cannot experience the exuberant vibrations of the unconditional love of Light without accepting the reality of Light.

What Is Light Awareness?

L ight awareness is my interpretation of the wisdom of God.

I interpret my awareness through my senses.

My interpretation of Light builds within the sensations of my heart chakra, which I call my Light awareness, my higher self, my highest mind perspective.

I began to build my awareness of Light when I found my connection to Light.

My senses are always on high alert, vibrating, moving, and interpreting.

Light intuits instant awareness in every situation.

I only accepted awareness by asking my higher self, my Light, direct yes or no questions about me initially and then asking general questions.

In my books *My Invisible World* and *How I Healed my Mind*, I laid out the many questions I needed to ask of myself and Light before I began to accept me, the Light aspect of my heart chakra.

Ideally, Light interpretation is Light-based, which means it is free from the influences of humanity's pain and learning.

The clarity of interpreted Light depends on the perspective of the person interpreting the Light.

I found my journey into my darkness very challenging, and as a result, I have developed many prayers that helped me enormously to survive my darkness. I share some of these prayers here, but I also share them throughout the book to help the reader clarify their meditations. I always write the prayers in the first person, so the reader is praying as they read.

I pray for courage and ask Light to show me the courage to sense and feel courageous.

I pray for inner strength by asking Light to help me feel the strength of Light to feel my inner strength.

I pray for inner strength to help me build self-discipline in my awareness and inner mind.

I pray for inspiration and insight; please help me identify my inspired and insightful thoughts and feelings and not dismiss them.

In Light awareness, there is no power, no powerlessness, no positive or negative thoughts, no knowledge, no hierarchy, no learning, and no lesser version of you. Instead, there is the wisdom of compassion and unconditional love.

Light awareness revealed the thoughts and behaviours that needed to heal within my mind. It also revealed that the absence of any self-awareness of Light within me held me in the darkness of ignorance and arrogance. Until I began my healing journey, I had no awareness.

It is challenging to build awareness of the Light within because the human being has no imprint of what Light awareness is. The mind will refute all efforts to connect to Light. That is why the work to achieve a connection to Light is repetitive and will appear weak or irrelevant from the mind's perspective. The initial mantra provides the imprint of the higher self, the Light within that is required to connect to Light.

The continuing meditations may appear the same, but the subtleties of Light will help you expand your connection to your higher self, the Light within.

What is Darkness?

As with Light, darkness exists within each of us.
I call this darkness the learned mind.

When I recognise the darkness within my thoughts and thinking, I pray to Light for the courage to help me face it and not be afraid.

I realised that darkness is not just within our minds, darkness is all-encompassing.

Light permitted me to recognise thought patterns that felt normal in my mind, but with a higher Light shining on them, I realised they were hostile and entrenched in powerful dogma. My thoughts were my darkness. While doing my development courses to become a healer, my mentor encouraged me to engage in Light. I thought I did. I assumed I did. Now I know that I connected to Light through my bravado entitled, assuming mind perspective.

In my entitled, assuming mind perspective, I saw the way to reach God was through spirit. A spirit guide was my new but automatically entitled assumed pathway to God. Unfortunately, this pathway to God was trapping me in the influences of darkness.

I also accepted that the mind is a powerful learned obstacle that prevents me from using my senses to con- nect to Light. Darkness cultivates the mind barriers automatically. For example, my bravado perspective automatically doubts the process of connecting to Light because it does not acknowledge that Light exists. This powerful thinking was a massive obstacle, along with other barriers that I had not imagined as blocks in my mind. Back in the early days when I sat in meditation, I blamed anything – the facilitator, the room, the heat, or the different personalities in the group as my reasons for failing to meditate. Instead, the obstacles were in my mindset, the complex web I had woven that represented me and the perspective I had built unknowingly as my mind and identity.

I needed to cultivate an inner discipline within my heart chakra to help me connect to Light. To help me build inner discipline and other boundaries, I use a breathing Light mantra during meditation to help me begin sensing and feeling Light.

I began with my intention to find my darkness by sitting in meditation, seeking the Light within. I get fantastic unconditional support from Light when I meditate. When I started to meditate a long time ago, I sat in a guided visualisation group for many years before acknowledging my mind's inner state, which revealed thoughts paralysed by fear.

It took several more years before I began to glimpse how Light worked with me. Only then could I finally shift the rigid thinking that kept me in denial of my fears, weakness, and victim thoughts.

As I accepted this revelation and began to transform some of my fears, I began questioning the value of a meditation that did not challenge me to find my darkness, worries, paralysis, and dysfunction.

One evening during meditation, I asked Light for a way I could see the obstacles and the barriers in my mind. Light intuited me to accept a meditation I call the Light within meditation.

The Light within meditation inspired me to seek my inner awareness of Light, which revealed my Light existence. I started to recognise the aura and how it generates, how the senses work, and how the chakras work within the system. I began to see the mind and how it works, and above all, I began to build awareness of Light within me.

As well as creating the Light within meditation, I have intuited and established the sensory boundaries of Light. I cultivated these sensory boundaries during my meditations throughout the years.

The first sensory boundary is truth. The truth interpreted from Light generates the boundary of truth that protects me from liars and manipulators, especially the liar and the manipulator within my automatic bravado-learned mind. The Light within meditation revealed the truth of me, not just the truth of Light, but the revelation of the darkness in my thoughts.

The unengaged Light or the shadowed Light within the mind works similarly to how the moon works. The moon only comes in the darkness of the night. So too does the hidden or denied Light suppressed within the mind. It usually manifests in a person's mind while they sleep through their dreams and visions.

The Light within meditation shines into the chakra system. The vibrancy of the highest Light that glistens like the brightest sun, allowing a person to engage their higher self and begin their self-healing journey. The Light from the highest vibration is invisible and subtle to the senses of the human being.

Why the Candle Flame?

The candle flame I use daily reflects an image of the highest Light vibration to me.

When I focus on the candle flame, several things occur.

The candle flame provides me with a colour and a structure for Light that I use in all meditations, healings, readings, and other work.

I use a candle flame as a symbol for the highest Light vibration during my work.

Focusing on the candle flame helps me unite my senses into the candle flame's single image of Light that allows me to attune to Light.

The candle flame I use in meditation provides a reflected flame of Light in the inner third eye space. It provides me with the inner space to focus the senses upwards from the Light in the heart chakra through this inner reflected flame in the third eye and to focus upwards through the crown chakra to reach and connect to the Light's highest vibration of the universe.

The candle flame provides the flame of Light to help the detachment from the learned and painful mind.

The candle flame gives me the presence of an unconditional friend as I work every day.

Focusing on the candle flame helps me to detach from all my learning.

Focusing on the candle flame helps me retrain my senses into a Light vibration.

Focusing on the candle flame helps me feel my senses in the weightlessness of Light and not feeling the weight of the mind's burden.

Focusing on the candle flame helps me remove the driving force of my thoughts that may be fuelling my pain and anxiety.

What are Light Boundaries?

L ight boundaries are the unique sensory tools you develop in your internal awareness as you interpret your unique wisdom from the highest Light vibrations.

Light boundaries must be your interpretation of Light, otherwise they will not work as you require them.

All auras are unique and individual because the aura's Light generates its unique nucleus of Light cells.

Each human being interprets and senses the highest vibration of Light from their aura's perspective. Each human being learns from the lower perspective of their bravado mind.

The Light awareness of each human being is unique to them.

The sensory Light boundaries of each human being are unique to their mind's perspective.

Protecting the Light existence in the heart chakra is necessary by engaging your self-created sensory boundaries of Light.

It is better for your awareness if you do not doubt your interpretations of Light.

The interpretations of Light will reveal the automatic learning of the bravado-learned conditioned mindset.

I accepted that I and every human being must detach from the bravado mind.

The perceived strengths of the mind are its learned barriers.

An example of a learned barrier is the instant ability to dismiss and disregard the feelings or opinions of other people, especially if they do not agree with the bravado mind's opinions.

Another example of a learned barrier is the power of the learned conditioned voice.

The learned barriers of the mind are lethal in their corruption of Light awareness.

I share a short synopsis of how I created my sensory boundaries, which may help you understand how to build your boundaries of Light.

The following text is an extract from 'What Are Boundaries of Light?' in my first book, My Invisible World.

What Are Boundaries of Light?

I intuitively created Light's boundaries as sensory energy tools of Light protection and security to help me safeguard the emergence of my Light existence within my heart chakra. These sensory boundaries also protect my intention to seek Light's clarity, seek Light's wisdom, express Light, interpret Light, facilitate Light, and write about Light.

When I accepted that I needed to develop boundaries to protect my Light awareness, I asked Light for an image to help me understand how to create boundaries. In meditation, I saw a picture of a beautiful rose with many petals in different colours. I realised that each rose petal has its purpose, but when all the petals are closed together, they create impenetrable protection for the core, the centre of the rose.

I interpreted the rose's protection as the impenetrable boundaries of Light protection for the emergence of the Light from within my heart chakra. My boundaries enable my Light awareness to grow and expand as the wisdom of Light filters into my senses, and ultimately, it builds into a new higher mind reality. When I began to engage in a

Light boundary during my healing sessions with clients, I started by creating a space between my client and me. I placed an imaginary candle flame in that space between us. This space worked wonderfully for me as I began to detach from the pain and emotion of the person seeking to heal. Of course, this discipline was desperately challenging for me to uphold. Nobody had told me about it or how to find it. I had no example to follow. There was no book to revert to when I needed to check for instructions. I interpret Light from Light as I heal and meditate. I write down my findings as my research. I use my research on myself in my self-healing. As my interpretations expand into insights that formulate solid thinking within my awareness, I use my research to heal and support my clients.

I began my internal work by listening and hearing my senses. I began to interpret their language of vibration. I did not use any external Light for this work; I drew on the Light of my heart chakra's resources. I gradually built-up insights into the many different boundaries that protect my Light awareness, which helps me not falter as I continue to build my Light awareness. I understand that each sensory boundary application is fundamental to the overall structure of Light protection. When I applied my boundaries to my mind, I recognised the spin of anxiety in my bravado mind. I saw my bravado perspective's full acceptance of the conditioned truth as truth versus what I was intuiting: the subtlety of Light's wisdom and its truth.

For this reason, I needed to understand the clarity of each sensory boundary. I also needed to engage the different Light boundaries as I require their protection from my bravado thoughts or external negative influences.

These are my interpreted individual boundaries of Light:

Grounding

Grounding is the sensory boundary I was most lax about because I was automatically familiar with it. I didn't pay it much attention as I thought I had learned about grounding during my meditation and healing courses. Finally, I understood that I was grounding my mind when I thought I was grounding my Light awareness, my higher myself.

People often told me, "Ground yourself; you are all over the place." I assumed I understood what they meant and would ground my mind into the earth just because I thought I needed to do that. I resisted the insights I received in meditation about grounding because I genuinely felt I had it covered.

When I accepted my insights on grounding, I gave them their proper evaluation of my Light awareness. As a result, I miraculously discovered two chakras at my feet that I needed to work through to complete the Light aura's reveal.

This insight and clarity also enabled me to realign my entire chakra system. I also saw it was my Light consciousness that I needed to ground into the earth. Including these two chakras opened my awareness to enable my intention to work internally for the first time. I focused my senses internally into my heart chakra and down through my solar plexus chakra, my sacral chakra, and my base chakra into my feet chakras. I then exited my senses from my feet chakras to enter the ground, to ground me in sensory roots similar to the roots of a giant oak tree, to help me sit or stand upright in Light awareness. After completing my lower chakras' grounding process, I refocused my senses on the Light of my heart chakra to align my upper chakras. I lifted my senses internally to travel from the Light in my heart chakra upwards through my throat chakra, through the third eye and to the crown chakras. I realised the revealed chakras are a restructure in Light consciousness without influence from external forces of energies. I am alone in accepting the responsibility for upholding the restructured chakra system and maintaining its Light vibrations.

Accepting the importance of grounding is an essential discipline that enables me to cultivate my Light awareness.

Trust

When I joined my first development meditation group, we needed help understanding the spirit's message about trust in the group. Not trust again, I often said to myself silently when spirit repeated its words about trust. Eventually, I interpreted that I had to cultivate my trust boundary, and each group member had to develop their trust boundaries. When I consciously sought to trust, I had to understand what trust meant. I asked myself what trust is, what it feels like, and what it means in my thoughts. I found my confidence in trusting by accepting that when I seek to trust Light, I am attempting to trust me, the Light aspect of my higher self. When I started to feel trust, I began to recognise the absence of trust in my mind, in my thoughts and feelings. I revealed the defensive barriers in my mind that unknowingly diverted my intention from seeking Light to automatically seeking the denser lower vibrations of my mind that urged me to seek the more robust trust structures within the symbols of the hierarchies of society.

My intention to seek Light and engage Light, coupled with my sense of trust, created the first step of my unique Light awareness.

Truth

Truth and trust were complex sensory boundaries for me to articulate within my intuition. Yet, I found them so similar in vibration that I needed to build them in tandem and separate their subtle differences. This difficulty in interpreting these boundaries revealed my mind's powerful dynamic to deny or suppress my unique individual truth and trust only my conditioned learned truth. The reveal of my mind was vital to expanding my healing insights as I continued to seek the truth of me, the Light that is me.

I began to glimpse and sense my trust as I built trust in my group facilitator. In feeling trust, I sensed my first antenna to the truth of my unique vibrations of Light. I felt this antenna as the tiniest whisper of awareness to change. I needed to acknowledge this insight and accept the need to begin healing. The whisper was not a powerful or powerless resourced voice; its subtleties were new to my senses. To hear it better, I needed to engage in the process of listening. The whisper is fleeting; it is difficult to hold and grasp because the power of my mind is only a thought away from suppressing this whisper. The awareness of the Light within expanded this whisper into an inner voice of wisdom. Trusting in the initial inner whisper of Light is the step that began the many steps into my inner reality of Light's truth.

The Light I attune to in meditation is the truth of God's Light that empowers me to accept my Light reality.

There is no deviation in this truth except for the faltering efforts within my newfound awareness to voice it and express it.

Trust and truth boundaries have become my definition as I evolve daily in my awareness of Light.

Responsibility

When I began to question responsibility, I instantly felt the burdened responsibility I carried in my learned mind that reflected my family's dynamic of collective responsibility.

I recognised my automatically learned responses to my family and extended family, work relationships, neighbours and neighbourhoods and even to my country and religion.

I became the observer of my automatic mindset, my automated actions, and my automatic reactions. I began to recognise the collective 'we' applied to the different learned responsibilities of my mind. I found I expressed 'we' in tandem with my automatic behaviour. For example, 'we have to' as I rushed around automatically to 'do' for others. 'We have to save them' as I worried about the potential loss. 'We have no choice' as I relented to bad or irresponsible choices made by others. 'We are beholden to them' as I was always grateful or indebted to others. 'We owe them' as I repaid dues repeatedly to people, I automatically thought I owed. 'We must be loyal' as I dared not betray, but I also dared others not to. 'We must not upset them' as I silently carried the secrets and the betrayal of other people. 'We have a duty to them' as I automatically felt obliged and bound to people. As I recognised these thought patterns, I consciously changed the 'we' thought in my thinking and actions to the 'I' thought. My boundaries of trust and truth supported my intention to seek individual responsibility. I developed a new thought application that gave me a new language of my senses. The language of my senses is Light-based vibrations without the influences of power or powerlessness. I express it as 'I feel, I believe, I trust, I sense, and I take responsibility.' As my new language grew within my conscious mind, my responsibilities became more evident.

I began to understand that the need for individual responsibilities lay within my heart and not in the collective consciousness. My newfound awareness permitted many insights into my mind. I eventually understood that I needed to take full responsibility for my thoughts, feelings, and how I lived my life.

Its burden manifested as physical anxiety that weighed down my shoulders and back, which closed my throat chakra. It took me a while to understand the truth of my responsibility.

I have entirely accepted that I am the only person that can heal my mind of its learned responsibility. I have entirely accepted responsibility for my mind by accepting responsibility for my life so far and accepting that my thoughts, whether rational or irrational, were me and created by me.

Respect

When I began my spiritual healing career, particularly when facilitating meditation groups, I repeatedly spoke of the need for respect. I accepted that I did not understand respect. Eventually, I looked it up in the dictionary for a meaning I truly understood and built the foundations of my new awareness. My learned understanding of respect seemed to apply outward towards others and society. I observed how I asked for respect from others, for people and buildings, but I never asked for personal respect. I found it challenging to apply respect to myself. Eventually, I understood I needed to flip my collective mental understanding of respect inwards to protect my heart, truth, and my Light aspect. I began by asking several questions. For example, Do I respect myself as I respect other people? Do I hold myself with respect when I am expressing myself? Do I respect that part of me that is an aspect of Light? Is my expression reflective of my respect for Light? Are my thoughts reflective of my respect for Light? Are my feelings reflective of my respect for Light? If I respect myself, why is my mind in a persistent state of conflict and regression? If I respect myself, why am I accepting disrespect from others in all its guises?

I dedicated my intention to providing respectful, safe spaces for people when I facilitate my meditation groups. A sense of respect is paramount when they begin to take the crunch steps to build their self-awareness and self-expression. The truth is a massive component of respect. Respect is a fundamental, essential foundation stone that supports a connection to the Light of the heart chakra without a falter or doubt before the process of evolving in Light can begin for a person. As I understood respect and its boundaries, I began to recognise my ignorance, control and manipulation in my thinking and thoughts.

As my Light awareness improves and expands, respect becomes apparent in my expression, intention, purpose, and behaviour. When people challenge me about my work, I have gradually learned how to express how I feel, hear, sense, see, etc. I know, instinctively, that these expressions are an indisputable truth, my truth. When others challenge my truth, I have learned to respect the reasons for their challenge, and I do not always feel the need to engage their opinions.

Honour

What did honour mean in my mind?

Did my learning about honour apply only to a society of powerful hierarchies?

As I sought to find honour in my thoughts, I recognised that I believed honour was for others, not me. I accepted that I needed to learn to honour my self-worth, to honour my truth, to honour my intention and my ability to heal. I especially needed to honour other people. I needed to honour their reactions to me in whatever vibration they came. I needed to honour that place where vulnerable people find themselves in times of emotional crisis. I needed to honour their truth even when it may be the opposite of mine.

As my Light awareness expands, I recognise that I am self-honouring, self-respecting, and self-validating the Light within my heart. I heal and release my learned mind from this reality in my Light awareness.

Acceptance

Acceptance is a gift from God. Unfortunately, humanity, including myself, finds it very difficult to accept unconditional gifts.

I found acceptance within my mind by consciously seeking non-acceptance-based thoughts and changing them. I have spent many years recognising my non-acceptance of myself within my mind. When I engaged the Light within my heart chakra, I instantly saw the necessity to accept Light's qualities that I was beginning to interpret as my boundaries. In my awareness, I fully accept my uniqueness in Light, my self-governance through Light, my autonomy within Light, and my expression through Light. I endeavour to live my life in this reality of Light, and I pray to Light that I find the confidence to hear the voice of Light to help me in my demise when my life as Lucy Devine ends and to empower me not to regress to my learned fears and learned automatic prayers.

Intention

The tool of my intention is the sensory boundary tool I have developed within my Light awareness to connect my senses to Light instantly. I unite my intention, free will, and senses, which I call focusing the senses. Focusing the senses allows me to explore higher vibrations of Light, but it also helps me regress safely in my mind when I need to self-heal.

From my Light awareness perspective, I revealed the lack of intention in the automatic mental barriers within my learned bravado mind.

I fully accept that my intention must be a conscious choice, and it is not something I can learn and recite when

I need to connect to my higher self. However, my intention to instantly connect to my Light awareness ensures I connect to Light and God every time.

Purpose

My purpose is another sensory tool of my Light awareness. It resembles a vehicle because it supports my intention to stay connected to Light. As the universal Light's vibrations and dimensions unfold during my meditations and healing experiences, I understand why purpose is essential in my work.

Passivity in my thoughts and emotions formed my mental paralysis internally for a long time.

My purpose was to have a quiet life, not be argumentative, and ensure peace and happiness for others.

As my awareness of Light expanded, my purpose became a conscious functioning tool in every thought, action, and reaction. My purpose became my existence of why I live. I have become purposeful in transmitting and sharing Light.

I consciously use my Light awareness for healing, insight, and no other reason.

My purpose in seeking Light has been to understand Light, and by understanding Light and how it works, I purposefully share it unconditionally.

Compassion

I express compassion in my care for people as I help them recognise their pain and vulnerabilities. I sit in my chair to listen and hear people in my compassionate awareness.

I validate feelings, thoughts and emotions as I help them reveal their invisible pain existences.

Compassion from my heart means I must share the Light at its highest vibration without my need to feel or own the emotion or the pain of my working situation. Therefore, I had to initially develop compassionate care for myself and my pain which helped me accept and validate my vulnerabilities.

My compassion means I understand and care about my actions and reactions towards myself and outwardly to other people, situations, disasters, emergencies, and conflicts that affect people's lives.

Empathy

My empathy means a sharing of the highest Light vibrations of unconditional love. Empathy is not a learned thought or emotion, and I accept that I cannot teach empathy.

My empathy does not involve tears, pity, sacrifice, or suffering. It does not include my telling or knowing, nor does it require any part of power or assertive behaviour. Instead, I silently and invisibly share my heart chakra's unconditional love with people as they travel on their life's journeys. I never claim to know people's feelings and emotions.

Initially, I was confused about compassion and empathy.

The difference was subtle and indistinguishable in my awareness until I recognised occasions when I over-extended my healing intention beyond my boundary of

Light. Then, I began to see when I expected responses of recognition or gratefulness.

I understand I must always be without the need for recognition, acclaim, or applause from the public audience for my work.

Humility

The humility I learned and understood from my earliest tender years is drawn from the image of the mother of Jesus, on her knees at the foot of the cross, carrying the crucified body of her dead son.

This humility determined the power of my sacrificial thoughts embedded in my mind that kept me on my knees without self-confidence or self-esteem until I got the sense to stand up in my mid-forties.

This humility was an invisible automatic weapon of sacrifice with which I wounded myself internally daily. My wounds were forever festering in different ways: in physical pain, mental distress, emotional upset, or spiritual fear.

These wounds were pierced automatically by my family, friends and society's disrespectful, dishonouring, irresponsible actions and reactions toward me.

More importantly, my disrespectful, dishonouring, and irresponsible thoughts, actions, and reactions toward me deeply hurt me.

I began to see my thinking pattern, where I denied or ignored these wounds' existence within my mind.

However, God's gift of synchronicity crashed into my life many times, forcing me to ask questions about myself and my relationships with others. The answers to my many questions eventually helped me recognise the thoughts that locked me into my denied invisible automatic victim suffering. As I began to heal these thoughts and change my feelings, I began to lift myself both up from my knees and lift my mind vibration. I began to take full responsibility for my actions and my reactions. I began to build a Light awareness of who I am as a Light aspect of God, my higher self.

The piercing efforts of others' actions hurt me less and gradually faded as my awareness and boundaries allowed me to detach from the bravado thoughts that would have me wound in return.

My humility is now a sensory Light tool.

I feel it with a person or situation that inspires me to feel the presence of God, either in his many glorious aspects of Light or in any of the hurt and wounded people I see and meet.

Detachment

Detachment is another unconditional gift from God that humanity finds very challenging to accept.

Detachment is an essential sensory boundary of Light in the evolving process.

I use a candle flame image to ensure I detach my awareness of Light from my mind and the powerful learning from the collective consciousness. I highly recommend using this Light symbol to help you detach from your mind and the collective consciousness.

If you intend to detach from a situation, a person, a family dynamic, a relationship, a thought, an emotion, or a spirit presence, place an image of a candle flame between you and the situation.

You must observe if your mind and body respond to the detachment process.

The observance will provide you with your unique truth about any situation, and the truth can quell your fears and doubts as you grow in confidence in your Light awareness.

When my mentor suggested to aspiring spiritual healers that learning to detach was the key to healing, I became confused and in flux. I fell into my mental trap of assuming that I understood his meaning when he asked us for detachment. In my mind, I visualised detachment as a physical distance, aloneness, or a cold, uncaring demeanour. I automatically imagined myself practising this detachment from my family. This thought alone spun me into the resistance of detachment as I knew I could not stop loving and caring for them. My mental action of flipping into understanding detachment's resistance led me into defensive thoughts, defensive language, and irrational resistance to control my mind and all I thought I knew.

I sat in many meditation groups, conflicted in my mind. I fought the inspiration in my awareness, revealing new understandings of love and acceptance. My conflict was not visual to my peers as I did not entertain that I may have misunderstood my understanding of detachment.

Eventually, I accepted my assumption that I knew the meaning of detachment was my block, not alone in my thoughts but in my emotions. It was also a significant block in developing my spiritual healing channel.

Ironically, my practice of spiritual healing revealed my insights into this detachment practice that I now call the greatest gift from God that I or any individual, can ask for and receive.

Courage

Courage is another tool of Light that helps people stand-still in their Light awareness and face the fear-based reality of their minds.

It is another essential sensory Light boundary. I use prayers to help me find courage when I need to not run from my fears and connect to Light and God. I needed and still need many prayers in my daily life. Many prayers of courage helped sustain me in Light and its strength and compassion when I faced many difficult, harsh and painful times I experienced.

I needed the courage to give conscious expression to these emotions. I also needed the courage to trust my articulation and interpretation of this new language of Light.

I wrote these prayers as I required them:

Please give me the courage to say what I believe is my truth.

Please give me the courage to listen.

Please give me the courage to stand still in my grounded Light awareness and not run to the hiding places within my mind.

Please give me the courage to remember that I am an aspect of Light.

Please give me the courage to voice my Light awareness when I feel challenged or pressured to agree with the collectively conditioned mindset.

Please give me the courage to face experiences and challenges and to recognise the pain.

Please give me the courage to release this pain and not suppress it or deny it, as is the habit of my learned behaviour.

Please give me the courage to love unconditionally. I have only loved conditionally; please give me the courage to release these conditions.

Please give me the courage not to control others with what I believe is my Light awareness.

Please give me the courage to detach from my anger.

Please give me the insight to not speak in anger.

Please give me the courage to continue to step forward, especially when I feel like not committing myself or my intention to that next step.

Expression

Expression is another essential sensory boundary of Light.

As I expand my awareness, I realise that I must express my voice and not suppress or deny it. When I suppress or deny my voice, I give people my power.

I clearly remember how I choked when my mentor asked me to facilitate a meditation group for the first time. The idea that I would facilitate a group of strangers triggered huge anxieties and inadequacies in my mind. I was so grateful that my mentor agreed to sit and support me that first night. I knew I was apt to do a runner and dart for the stairs as the challenges of the night became apparent in my mind and body. I sat there sweating profusely and visibly shaking, forgetting everything I had built as my awareness, allowing my racing mind automatically to take flight in fear and panic. I tried to control my mind by clasping my hands tightly together. His presence supported me in strength and courage, and I finished the group that night by thanking God that we all survived it. I was also aware that I received enormous support from my guides and the group. I looked to my mentor for praise; he was positive in his words of support, but just enough for me not to ignore my feelings of inadequacy and my fears and anxieties of the night. I had many years of meditating experience but facilitating was a different kettle of fish, as I was now required to share and speak of my insights and understanding of spirit, spirit guides and God. I had to begin to talk and assert my truth to strangers. That night

I left the centre feeling frustrated and greatly challenged in myself. I felt very sorry for myself as I thought I had healed many of these fears within my mind.

I had never exposed or challenged myself in this way before. It was a terrifying experience as I battled my automatic urges to run away and hide against my recognition of my need to learn to facilitate. As a trainee facilitator of Light, I knew I had to trust myself to speak the truth in every situation and to every question during the meditation. I also had to believe that my intuition, as enlightened as it was, would not cloud or be overwhelmed by my fears and anxieties. I was similar to a toddler in a vibration reality. I recognised the times when I'd shine in Light, and then there were times I realised when my intention and focus fell through the automatic escape hatch into my mind.

On these occasions, when I defaulted to my comfort zones, I trusted that group members were supported sufficiently by the presence of Light and their spirit guides.

This support manifested in many ways from the invisible world of spirit and Light until my self-esteem and self-confidence emerged. My Light boundaries ensured I did not fluctuate to the panders of my bravado mind.

How to Connect to the Light Within?

T he Light within is subtle in its vibration and is, therefore, not easy to sense. Moreover, when I glimpsed
the Light initially, it was fleeting and disappeared almost
instantly. On the other hand, I found it straightforward to
sense the denser conditioned energies of the solar plexus
because they felt 'strong' to my automatic bravado mindset.

The automatic, instantaneous familiarity and acceptance of the denser energies of the lower chakras are the
most potent reason to detach from the bravado mind.

The detachment from the bravado mind allows people
to build their Light awareness by accepting what they feel
and sense as authentic inspiration. The detachment process also enables a person to realign the spiritual chakras,
the crown chakra, the third eye chakra, the throat chakra,
the heart chakra, the lower chakras of the mind, the solar plexus chakra, sacral chakra, base chakra and the feet
chakras into a Light awareness.

Understanding the need to detach from your learned
interpretation of spirit is essential because spirit is the reflected impression of humanity's mind, which can be dark
and painfully challenging to disengage.

It is difficult to detach from the mind as we have individually built our minds into controlling survival tools.

The Light within meditation is initially a fundamentally empowering experience for an individual.

It permits a person to glow in the brightness of their unique Light within.

The Light contains the wisdom of the wholeness of God in its sensations.

During meditation, each person must interpret Light's sensations into their unique and individual truth of Light that forms the basis of their enlightened mind or Light awareness.

Each person must apply the Light boundaries to protect their Light's emergence. The Light within meditation is a unique and individual experience of the higher consciousness, or as I have called it, the Light within, the higher self.

The Way To Connect To Light?

The basic but most important message of the Light within meditation you need to grasp is that you need to generate a reflected light to enable you to connect to the Light within.

The first step to begin seeking Light is to light a candle.

The flame of the candle provides the symbol of the highest Light vibration.

The flame permits you to find, reveal and connect the aura, the chakras and the Light within and it also provides the channel to connect to the highest vibration of the universal Light.

What does 'focus the senses mean'?

'Focus the senses' is a term I use to help people internally unite their intention, free will, and senses into one action during meditation. I use 'focus the senses' throughout my meditations as it provides an intention for the senses to connect instantly to the highest vibration of Light.

Your senses are seeing, hearing, touch, taste, smell, and the aura's unique intuition.

(See 'What Are the Senses' chapter in *My Invisible World*)

What is the purpose of connecting to Light?

The purpose of the Light within meditation is to provide the inner discipline to seek and feel Light and grow into the awareness of the higher self. When a person accepts the Light reality within the heart chakra, it is easier to get the existence of the aura, chakras, a chakra system, and the energies of the entire physical body and begin the journey into self-healing.

These are some of the results when connecting to the Light Within.

➤ A person seeks their reflected self as an image of Light.

➤ A person expands their sensory awareness of Light.

➤ A person opens up their sensory awareness of the self.

➤ A person feels the existence of their higher self, the Light within.

➤ A person experiences freedom from their learned perspective.

➤ A person experiences joy.

➤ A person experiences peace.

➤ A person feels unconditional love within themselves.

➤ A person may feel a release from the heavy burdens of their mind for the first time.

➤ A person finds the courage to begin to unravel their mind's reality.

➤ A person finds the courage to exercise choice and free will.

➤ A person learns about boundaries.

- A person identifies their mental barriers.
- A person learns how to realign their chakras.
- A person learns how to be present within their senses.
- A person fully aware of Light feels empowered and centred within themselves.
- In connecting to the Light within, you are not creating anything new.
- The aura already exists because it creates at conception. You are not trying to alter the Light vibration, which is the imprint of the Light within, which is your birthright, and you alone can claim it.
- The Light within the heart chakra already exists.
- The aura, the chakras, and the suppressed mind all exist.

What would you see if I asked you to close your eyes and focus inwards on yourself? It is darkness, and darkness is the vibration of the mind. For this reason, it is challenging for your mind to release the senses to seek a Light existence.

What does the Mantra Meditation mean?

The mantra meditation is an essential working technique I require from you in all future meditations that will help you to evolve into the awareness of the higher self, the Light within.

The mantra meditation is a specific breathing technique that enhances awareness and the conscious connection to Light enabling a person to expand their sensory awareness.

The mantra uses the natural flow of the breath to maintain a focus and connection to Light.

The mantra discipline combines the conscious inhalation of breath and the Light from the candle and the exhalation of breath and Light.

Using the mantra works in several ways for the user of the mantra.

1. It retrains the senses to seek a Light reflection.
2. It helps the user to make positive, empowered decisions by seeking their Light.
3. It helps the user observe thoughts and not engage them.

4. It detaches the user from the vibrations of the learned familiarity of the bravado mind.

5. It creates a Light space within the heart chakra that permits the user to sense, feel and interpret their Light existence and observe their thoughts.

6. It helps the user build inner strength and discipline by recognising how their thoughts distract them from their Light meditation. The user must instantly detach from the distraction of thoughts and reconnect their senses to Light by refocusing on their Light mantra.

7. It helps the user recognise when their thoughts diminish their meditating efforts.

8. It helps the user observe their mind working and decide to detach from their mental power by focusing on the Light mantra.

9. It helps the user recognise the driving force of their mind to survive the meditation by recognising their mind's fears about the meditation.

10. It helps the user recognise their sense of powerlessness and instead detach from the sense of powerlessness to focus on the Light mantra.

11. It helps the user sense empowerment by exercising choice and sticking to it.

12. It helps the user understand and accept that they are not their emotions or learning by sensing and accepting Light.

13. It helps users trust their feelings and not suppress or ignore them.
14. It inspires users to create and build their awareness of Light.
15. It helps users detach from their peers' opinions and thoughts and the collective society.
16. It helps users advance their Light awareness by seeking higher Light vibrations.

The Mantra Meditation

The Mantra Meditation is the first meditation. It allows everyone to recreate and ignite the internal imprint of their Light being, their higher self, and their Light within. This imprint is a triangle of Light between the heart, the third eye and the throat chakras.

The mantra is your lifetime sensory tool that enables you to hold and expand your Light awareness perspective by detaching and disconnecting from your thoughts and emotions.

The purpose of the mantra meditation is to train your senses and your inner mind perspective to seek the Light instead of connecting to the sensory learned pain of the mind.

The mantra meditation is the essential practised inner discipline of applying boundaries of detachment and finding a unique truth within Light awareness.

The mantra is a repetitive action and reaction in your breathing. It takes time, purpose, and intention to become comfortable with it.

You are disconnecting your senses from the learned bravado mind and reconnecting them to Light.

The mantra meditation is the foundation for all your future meditations and healings. Therefore, it is vital to help you build your self-esteem, trust, and self-confidence in this triangle of Light by practising the mantra daily for at least ten minutes.

Sitting in a room with a candle flame is the ideal way to develop your mantra technique.

However, sitting in a garden and looking at grass, you can practice the mantra by breathing in the green as you focus on the grass. If you are looking at the sky, you can practice your mantra by breathing in the blue sky or breathing in the space you feel between you and the sky. You can practice the mantra by breathing in the sun's rays while sitting in the sunshine. Finally, you can practice your mantra by breathing in the sea's smell, colour or sound if you are looking out to the sea.

If you witness an argument, you can practice your mantra by instantly detaching from the argument by placing an imaginary candle flame between you and the argument and practising the meditation of breathing Light.

The mantra will enable you to make better decisions for yourself minute-to-minute. You can stop worrying by simply becoming conscious of what your mind automatically engages in and instead consciously breath the mantra technique.

The discipline of the mantra breathing stops the worrying instantly.

Always dedicate your meditation to Light, even if doing it for a few minutes.

Begin your journey of turning the senses inwards by gazing outwards at the candlelight,

The mantra's technique focuses entirely on your breathing that combines the candle flame with the inhalation and exhalation of your breath.

All your breathing must inhale through the nose and exhale through the mouth.

Breathe in Light and breathing out Light is counted as one in-breath.

To start your meditation:

1. Find a room where you will not be disturbed for at least ten minutes.
2. Place a candle on a table in front of you.
3. As you light it, dedicate your intention to connect to the highest Light.

For the best results from the meditation, it is best to sit on a chair. Place the feet firmly on the ground. The small of the back pushed into the support of the chair. Loosely fold your hands on your lap. The mantra is a very slow and repetitive discipline to acquire.

As you light your candle, dedicate your intention to seeking Light from the highest vibration of the universe for your healing and self-awareness.

With open eyes, focus your senses outwards toward the candle flame. Then, in your mind's eye, observe the natural internal flow of your breathing.

Allow your focus to follow the natural rhythm of the breath.

Effortlessly merge the breathing in of air and the candle flame light as one action.

Begin to consciously breathe in light and breathe out light.

As you focus on your breathing, begin to voice the action internally.

Breathe in light, say to yourself, 'Breathe in light.'

As you breathe out light, say to yourself, 'Breathe out light.'

The unified breathing in of air, of the candle flame, and the internal use of the words must become one action of the senses that develop the rhythm of the mantra.

As you breathe in light, you say to yourself, 'Breathe in light.'

As you breathe out light, you say to yourself, 'Breathe out the light.'

> Breathe in light as you follow your breath up through the nose. Breathe out light as you exhale through the mouth.
>
> Breathe in light as you follow your breath up through the nose. Breathe out light as you exhale through the mouth.
>
> Breathe in light as you follow your breath up through the nose. Breathe out light as you exhale through the mouth.

Continue to look at the candle flame and repeat.

Breathe in light as you follow your breath up through the nose. Breathe out light as you exhale through the mouth.

Breathe in light as you follow your breath up through the nose. Breathe out light as you exhale through the mouth.

Breathe in light as you follow your breath up through the nose. Breathe out light as you exhale through the mouth.

Continue to look outwards at the candle flame and repeat.

Breathe in light as you follow your breath up through the nose. Breathe out light as you exhale through the mouth.

Breathe in light as you follow your breath up through the nose. Breathe out light as you exhale through the mouth.

Breathe in light as you follow your breath up through the nose. Breathe out light as you exhale through the mouth.

Close your eyes. Continue breathing in the rhythm of the mantra breathing.

Roll the eyes inwards towards the bridge of the nose area, and you are looking for a reflected candle flame that may appear in your third eye space. With the eyes closed, continue to breathe, and say the mantra for three in-breaths.

> Breathe in light as you follow your breath up through the nose. And breathe out light, as you exhale through the mouth.
>
> Breathe in light as you follow your breath up through the nose. And breathe out light, as you exhale through the mouth.
>
> Breathe in light as you follow your breath up through the nose. And breathe out light, as you exhale through the mouth.

Open your eyes. Focus your senses outwards to the candle flame. Commence the mantra breathing for five in-breaths to reconnect your senses to Light.

Use your fingers to count the in-breaths. Gently tap a finger for each in-breath on your thigh.

> Breathe in light as you follow your breath up through the nose. Breathe out light as you exhale through the mouth.

Breathe in light as you follow your breath up through the nose. Breathe out light as you exhale through the mouth.

Breathe in light as you follow your breath up through the nose. Breathe out light as you exhale through the mouth.

Breathe in light as you follow your breath up through the nose. Breathe out light as you exhale through the mouth.

Breathe in light as you follow your breath up through the nose. Breathe out light as you exhale through the mouth.

Close your eyes. Continue breathing in the rhythm of the mantra breathing.

Roll the eyes inwards towards the bridge of the nose area, and you are looking for a reflected candle flame that may appear in your third eye space. With the eyes closed, continue to breathe, and say the mantra for three in-breaths.

Breathe in light as you follow your breath up through the nose. Breathe out light as you exhale through the mouth.

Breathe in light as you follow your breath up through the nose. Breathe out light as you exhale through the mouth.

Breathe in light as you follow your breath up through the nose. Breathe out light as you exhale through the mouth.

Open your eyes. Focus your senses outwards to the candle flame. Commence the mantra breathing for five in-breaths to reconnect your senses to Light.

Breathe in light as you follow your breath up through the nose. Breathe out light as you exhale through the mouth.
Breathe in light as you follow your breath up through the nose. Breathe out light as you exhale through the mouth.
Breathe in light as you follow your breath up through the nose. Breathe out light as you exhale through the mouth.
Breathe in light as you follow your breath up through the nose. Breathe out light as you exhale through the mouth.
Breathe in light as you follow your breath up through the nose. Breathe out light as you exhale through the mouth.

Close your eyes. Continue breathing in the rhythm of the mantra breathing.

Roll the eyes inwards towards the bridge of the nose area, and you are looking for a reflected candle flame that may appear in your third eye space. With the eyes closed, continue to breathe, and say the mantra for three in-breaths.

> Breathe in light as you follow your breath up through the nose. Breathe out light as you exhale through the mouth.
> Breathe in light as you follow your breath up through the nose. Breathe out light as you exhale through the mouth.
> Breathe in light as you follow your breath up through the nose. Breathe out light as you exhale through the mouth.

Open your eyes. Focus your senses outwards to the candle flame. Commence the mantra breathing for five in-breaths to reconnect your senses to Light.

> Slowly breathe in light as you follow your breath up through the nose. Breathe out light as you exhale through the mouth.
> Slowly breathe in light as you follow your breath up through the nose. Breathe out light as you exhale through the mouth.
> Slowly breathe in light as you follow your breath up through the nose. Breathe out light as you exhale through the mouth.
> Slowly breathe in light as you follow your breath up through the nose. Breathe out light as you exhale through the mouth.

Slowly breathe in light as you follow your breath up through the nose. Breathe out light as you exhale through the mouth.

Close your eyes. Continue breathing in the rhythm of the mantra breathing.

Roll the eyes inwards towards the bridge of the nose area, and you are looking for a reflected candle flame that may appear in your third eye space. With the eyes closed, continue to breathe, and say the mantra for three in-breaths.

Slowly breathe in light as you follow your breath up through the nose. Breathe out light as you exhale through the mouth.
Slowly breathe in light as you follow your breath up through the nose. Breathe out light as you exhale through the mouth.
Slowly breathe in light as you follow your breath up through the nose. Breathe out light as you exhale through the mouth.

Open your eyes. Focus your senses outwards to the candle flame. Commence the mantra breathing for five in-breaths to reconnect your senses to Light.

Slowly breathe in light as you follow your breath up through the nose. Breathe out light as you exhale through the mouth.

Slowly breathe in light as you follow your breath up through the nose. Breathe out light as you exhale through the mouth.

Slowly breathe in light as you follow your breath up through the nose. Breathe out light as you exhale through the mouth.

Slowly breathe in light as you follow your breath up through the nose. Breathe out light as you exhale through the mouth.

Slowly breathe in light as you follow your breath up through the nose. Breathe out light as you exhale through the mouth.

Close your eyes. Continue breathing in the rhythm of the mantra breathing.

Roll the eyes inwards towards the bridge of the nose area, and you are looking for a reflected candle flame that may appear in your third eye space. With the eyes closed, continue to breathe, and say the mantra for three in-breaths.

Slowly breathe in light as you follow your breath up through the nose. Breathe out light as you exhale through the mouth.

Slowly breathe in light as you follow your breath up through the nose. Breathe out light as you exhale through the mouth.

Slowly breathe in light as you follow your breath up through the nose. Breathe out light as you exhale through the mouth.

Open your eyes. Focus your senses outwards to the candle flame. Commence the mantra breathing for five in-breaths to reconnect your senses to Light.

Slowly breathe in light as you follow your breath up through the nose. Breathe out light as you exhale through the mouth.

Slowly breathe in light as you follow your breath up through the nose. Breathe out light as you exhale through the mouth.

Slowly breathe in light as you follow your breath up through the nose. Breathe out light as you exhale through the mouth.

Slowly breathe in light as you follow your breath up through the nose. Breathe out light as you exhale through the mouth.

Slowly breathe in light as you follow your breath up through the nose. Breathe out light as you exhale through the mouth.

Close your eyes. Continue breathing in the rhythm of the mantra breathing.

Roll the eyes inwards towards the bridge of the nose area. You are looking for a reflected candle flame that may appear in your third eye space behind the bridge of the nose. With the eyes closed, continue to breathe, and say the mantra for three in-breaths.

> Slowly breathe in light as you follow your breath up through the nose. Breathe out light as you exhale through the mouth.
> Slowly breathe in light as you follow your breath up through the nose. Breathe out light as you exhale through the mouth.
> Slowly breathe in light as you follow your breath up through the nose. Breathe out light as you exhale through the mouth.

Open your eyes. Focus your senses outwards to the candle flame. Commence the mantra breathing for five in-breaths to reconnect your senses to Light.

Continue to consciously slow down the breathing by counting to five as you breathe in, counting to five as you hold your breath, and counting to five as you exhale through the mouth.

> Slowly breathe in light for a count of five. Hold it in your lungs for a count of five. Breathe out light for a count of five as you exhale through the mouth.
> Slowly breathe in light for a count of five. Hold it in your lungs for a count of five. Breathe out

light for a count of five as you exhale through the mouth.

Slowly breathe in light for a count of five. Hold it in your lungs for a count of five. Breathe out light for a count of five as you exhale through the mouth.

Slowly breathe in light for a count of five. Hold it in your lungs for a count of five. Breathe out light for a count of five as you exhale through the mouth.

Slowly breathe in light for a count of five. Hold it in your lungs for a count of five. Breathe out light for a count of five as you exhale through the mouth.

Close your eyes. Continue breathing in the rhythm of the mantra breathing.

Roll the eyes inwards towards the bridge of the nose area. You are looking for a reflected candle flame that may appear in your third eye space. With the eyes closed, continue to breathe, and say the mantra for three in-breaths.

Slowly breathe light up through the nose to reach the internal flame in your third eye chakra. Hold your breath in your lungs for a count of five. Slowly exhale light through the mouth for a count of five.

Slowly breathe light up through the nose to reach the internal flame in your third eye chakra. Hold your breath in your lungs for a count of five. Slowly exhale light through the mouth for a count of five.

Slowly breathe light up through the nose to reach the internal flame in your third eye chakra. Hold your breath in your lungs for a count of five. Slowly exhale light through the mouth for a count of five.

Open your eyes. Focus your senses outwards to the candle flame. Commence the mantra breathing for five in-breaths to reconnect your senses to Light.

Slowly breathe in light for a count of five, hold it in your lungs for a count of five. Breathe out light for a count of five as you exhale through the mouth.

Slowly breathe in light for a count of five, hold it in your lungs for a count of five. Breathe out light for a count of five as you exhale through the mouth.

Slowly breathe in light for a count of five, hold it in your lungs for a count of five. Breathe out light for a count of five as you exhale through the mouth.

Slowly breathe in light for a count of five, hold it in your lungs for a count of five. Breathe out light for a count of five as you exhale through the mouth.

Slowly breathe in light for a count of five, hold it in your lungs for a count of five. Breathe out light for a count of five as you exhale through the mouth.

Close your eyes. Continue breathing in the rhythm of the mantra breathing.

Roll the eyes inwards towards the bridge of the nose area. You are looking for a reflected candle flame that may appear in your third eye space. With the eyes closed, continue to breathe, and say the mantra for three in-breaths.

Slowly breathe light up through the nose to reach the internal flame in your third eye chakra. Hold your breath in your lungs for a count of five. Slowly exhale light through the mouth for a count of five.

Slowly breathe light up through the nose to reach the internal flame in your third eye chakra. Hold your breath in your lungs for a count of five. Slowly exhale light through the mouth for a count of five.

Slowly breathe light up through the nose to reach the internal flame in your third eye chakra. Hold your breath in your lungs for a count of five.

Slowly exhale light through the mouth for a count of five.

Open your eyes. Focus your senses outwards to the candle flame. Commence the mantra breathing for five in-breaths to reconnect your senses to Light.

Continue to consciously slow down the breathing by counting to five as you breathe in, counting to five as you hold your breath, and counting to five as you exhale through the mouth.

Slowly breathe in light for a count of five, hold it in your lungs for a count of five. Breathe out light for a count of five as you exhale through the mouth. Slowly breathe in light for a count of five, hold it in your lungs for a count of five. Breathe out light for a count of five as you exhale through the mouth.

Slowly breathe in light for a count of five, hold it in your lungs for a count of five. Breathe out light for a count of five as you exhale through the mouth.

Slowly breathe in light for a count of five, hold it in your lungs for a count of five. Breathe out light for a count of five as you exhale through the mouth. Slowly breathe in light for a count of five, hold it in your lungs for a count of five. Breathe out light for a count of five as you exhale through the mouth.

Close your eyes. Continue breathing in the rhythm of the mantra breathing.

Roll the eyes inwards towards the bridge of the nose area. You are looking for a reflected candle flame that may appear in your third eye space. With the eyes closed, continue to breathe, and say the mantra for three in-breaths.

Slowly breathe light up through the nose to reach the internal flame in your third eye chakra. Hold your breath in your lungs. Focus the light from the third eye chakra downwards to connect to the light in the heart chakra. Slowly exhale light through the mouth for a count of five.

Next, slowly breathe light up through the nose to reach the internal flame in your third eye chakra. Hold your breath in your lungs. Focus the light from the third eye chakra downwards to connect to the light in the heart chakra. Slowly exhale light through the mouth for a count of five.

Again, slowly breathe light up through the nose to reach the internal flame in your third eye chakra. Hold your breath in your lungs. Focus the light from the third eye chakra downwards to connect to the light in the heart chakra. Slowly exhale light through the mouth for a count of five.

Keep your eyes closed and repeat.

Slowly breathe light up through the nose to reach the internal flame in your third eye chakra. Hold your breath in your lungs. Focus the light from the third eye chakra downwards to connect to the light in the heart chakra. Slowly exhale light through the mouth for a count of five.

Next, slowly breathe light up through the nose to reach the internal flame in your third eye chakra. Hold your breath in your lungs. Focus the light from the third eye chakra downwards to connect to the light in the heart chakra. Slowly exhale light through the mouth for a count of five.

Again, slowly breathe light up through the nose to reach the internal flame in your third eye chakra. Hold your breath in your lungs. Focus the light from the third eye chakra downwards to connect to the light in the heart chakra. Slowly exhale light through the mouth for a count of five.

Keep your eyes closed and repeat.

Slowly breathe light up through the nose to reach the internal flame in your third eye chakra. Hold your breath in your lungs. Focus the light from the third eye chakra downwards to connect to the light in the heart chakra. Slowly exhale light through the mouth for a count of five.

Next, slowly breathe light up through the nose to reach the internal flame in your third eye chakra. Hold your breath in your lungs. Focus the light from the third eye chakra downwards to connect to the light in the heart

chakra. Slowly exhale light through the mouth for a count of five.

Again, slowly breathe light up through the nose to reach the internal flame in your third eye chakra. Hold your breath in your lungs. Focus the light from the third eye chakra downwards to connect to the light in the heart chakra. Slowly exhale light through the mouth for a count of five.

Open your eyes. Focus your senses outwards to the candle flame. Commence the mantra breathing for four in-breaths to reconnect your senses to Light.

Breathe in light up through the nose. Exhale light through the mouth.

Breathe in light up through the nose. Exhale light through the mouth.

Breathe in light up through the nose. Exhale light through the mouth.

Breathe in light up through the nose. Exhale light through the mouth.

Close your eyes. Continue in the rhythm of the gentle mantra breathing for ten in-breaths. Extend this time as confidence in your mantra technique grows.

If thoughts or external noise break into your meditation, breathe them out with the next exhale and continue with mantra breathing.

If you lose count of your breathing, Light will prompt you to cease your meditation, immediately stop your mantra breathing and become conscious of your body and mind by stretching your arms and hands, feet and toes. Open your eyes. Check how you feel and accept your feelings.

It is vital to hold on to your Light awareness after meditation. You do this by grounding yourself in light.

Grounding

Grounding is an exercise to facilitate light awareness within the mind. You do this by placing a hand over the crown chakra at the top of your head while you gaze at the candle flame and imagine that the hand is a beacon of Light shining its light right down the entire chakra system exiting through chakras at the soles of the feet. Observe the light develop roots deep within the earth's energies, helping you to remain in a Light awareness until the next time.

Insights that help build your Awareness of your Meditation Technique

T he mantra technique must become as natural as breathing in your inner awareness. It must become your default, even in harrowing and challenging situations.

Refrain from letting your mind tell you that the mantra is not working or that the whole process is too dull.

Of course, the mind will reason that because it doesn't want to lose control.

The repetition of breathing will help you build your inner self-discipline to focus your senses and stay focused on your purpose, which is to connect and stay connected to Light.

The mantra technique will help you to detach from your thoughts instantly.

The breathing technique will strengthen your senses to seek Light's awareness and to not default to the learning of the bravado mindset.

The breathing technique will give you confidence in your interpreting ability as you work with your senses in Light vibrations.

For beginners starting in meditation, a sense of Light is fleeting.

It isn't easy to get a sense of it because you are still seeking it through the mind, but it is my experience that Light always manifests for the seeker of Light.

It is the sense of Light you must be open to feeling, interpreting, and accepting as your Light.

Not getting disheartened or discouraged or believing this meditation is not for you is critical.

Please remember that you are beginning to take your first steps to sense your higher self. This action will challenge the mind, and the mind may endeavour to overshadow your efforts to change.

The meditation is for you.

So, persevere in your efforts to achieve your mantra technique for you.

Prayers for healing and Light Awareness

The following pages are insights and prayers to help you build your awareness of Light and your unique self.

I have written the prayers in the first person, so as you read them, you are reading them yourself.

It is best to use one prayer each time you meditate, as it is easier to sense or interpret the insight, intuition or inspired sensations, feelings or thoughts you may sense during meditation.

The insights I write about are the unique interpretations of Light that formulate to build a Light consciousness and a sensory awareness for a person. This Light awareness builds to become the evolving unique mindset supported by Light and created in Light.

The prayers I write are the little conversations that go on in the inner awareness of a person with their unique self, the Light within, as the person becomes conscious of the obstacles or pain they are about to face within their mind.

I must stress the importance of the mantra meditation to be practised regularly to develop confidence in your technique and to maintain your connection to the highest Light vibrations.

Insights that help build your Light Awareness

The Mantra Meditation

T he mantra needs to be your default when you feel challenged within your mind. You must use your mantra to instantly detach from the person or emotion threatening or upsetting you when you find yourself in difficult situations.

The Light we are seeking in the Light within meditation is subtle in vibration. Because of this subtlety, I discovered the many avenues my mind created to divert me from Light. After many years of meditation, I found my learned assumption in my mind that I was connecting to Light. Unfortunately, my awareness had dropped to my automatic learning, and because I believed my ego and didn't question it enough, it was diverting me from Light. My ego was shadowing my connection to Light through my fears and shadows.

I also discovered that I could not manipulate Light or control it.

If you are interested in building your Light awareness, you must engage with Light through your senses. I cannot emphasise enough how important it is to practice your mantra technique in your meditation.

The mantra technique is the key to this action.

Prayers for healing and Light Awareness

Light, please help me to sense Light so that I don't doubt the existence of Light.

Please help me sense Light so I can feel the Light in my heart chakra.

Light, please help me to recognise my awareness.

Light, please, help me to recognise the controlling influences within my thoughts.

Light, please help me to detach from this influence.

Please help me Light recognise my assumed thoughts that are invisibly and automatically controlling me.

Please help me recognise my fears and give me the strength to detach from them.

Insights that help build your Light Awareness

The Light Within

The first insight into the Light within meditation for you to accept is that you cannot learn about Light.

To find Light, you must seek Light and sense Light. Initially, you will feel vulnerable in the awareness of your senses as you begin to trust your Light sensations.

You must sense Light and trust the confidence in your Light awareness to accept these sensations.

You must refrain from bringing your learning or knowledge to support your vulnerabilities in your meditation. Likewise, you must not bring your religion's learning and deity to help support or validate your meditation.

You must not engage with fear whilst you meditate. If you sense fear or anxiety, please place a candle flame between your heart chakra and the fear and revert to your mantra breathing.

The Light, in its fullest of sensations, will support you.

Prayers for healing and Light Awareness

Light, please help me to detach entirely from my learning and my mind.

Please help me gain sincerity in my effort to sense Light.

Light, please help me to accept my intuition about Light.

Light, please help me not to doubt my intuition about Light.

Insights that help build your Light Awareness

Light

There are no future or past existences in Light.
Light is still.
Light is peace.
Light is supportive.
I connect to Light through the senses.
The senses emanate from the aura.
When I connected to Light.
I discovered that God exists within Light.
I discovered that God exists in darkness.

Insights that help build your Awareness of the Light Within

As your thoughts try to influence your focus when you meditate, you must remember you are not seeking to engage your power or your thoughts or learning. The reason you are meditating is to seek the wisdom of Light.

If you become aware of these intrusions, you must practice your detachment boundary to help you remain detached from your mind and be determined to reach the Light by reconnecting to your mantra breathing. It would be best to cultivate a determined focus to connect to Light within your awareness. You can build this focus to reach the Light by practising your mantra repeatedly.

If you cannot practice your mantra without using a candle flame to focus on, bring a candle flame up on your phone screen or computer screen or connect to the candle flame on my website. Please do not place obstacles in your way of practising your mantra.

It is your journey of exploring your sensory Light, your higher self. Nobody else must influence it or try to interfere with it.

Prayers for healing and Light Awareness

Light, please help me to find the truth within me.

Please help me trust Light and my Light awareness and not doubt my feelings.

Light, please help me to strengthen my intention to seek Light, because I am beginning to see when I automatically default to my lazy ways of non-thinking.

What is Self-Healing?

Self-healing occurs as you build your awareness of Light through meditation.

Self-healing is a conscious choice to live through the sensory awareness of Light.

Self-healing only occurs from a Light perspective.

Self-healing awareness cannot be assumed, entitled, or demanded by the seeker of healing.

The Light perspective and Light awareness intuit the self-correcting, self-balancing skills that retain a person in their self-generated Light awareness protected by the inspired self-created sensory boundary system.

As a self-healing and meditation facilitator, I list below my healing ethos to ensure everyone has clarity of my meditation and healing intention. It is particularly essential for any person endeavouring to self-heal and evolve.

This ethos may also help people understand how healing and self-healing may work for them.

When I sit in meditation or a healing session with clients, I sit, having tuned my senses to the highest vibration of Light.

I am the facilitator of Light, the support structure that enables a person to attune to their higher self, the Light within their heart chakra.

- I support a person in their intention to seek Light and in their effort to build a Light awareness.
- I support a person in their endeavour to connect to Light and in the revelation of their Light body.
- I cannot claim to be the Light that provides miracles for a person. I am just the facilitator of the Light.
- As a facilitator of Light, I cannot tell a person what to do or dictate their order.
- I cannot accept responsibility for other people's mindsets.
- I cannot approve or disapprove of the thinking of any mindset.
- I do not tell a person what is right or what is wrong.
- I cannot lift a person's pain, and I cannot claim that I can lift pain.
- I do not play manipulative, influential mind games in any of their hierarchies of either power or powerlessness.
- The mind, the ego, is the person's responsibility as it is their creation. Therefore, I stress to my clients the importance of accepting responsibility for their mindset to permit healing.
- I support a person seeking recognition of their mind and its revelations.
- I support a person in the transmutation of the reveal of their mind dynamic.
- I support a person in their endeavour to understand vibration.

- I support a person's effort to lift their mind's perspective.
- I accept the responsibility for a person's connection to their Light until they can accept and take responsibility.
- I support a person to explore the invisible world of spirit, provided they seek it from a Light perspective.
- I support people as they rescue the unknown or hidden parts of their bravado mindset.
- I accept responsibility for my interpretation of the reflected mind aspects.

As a facilitator of Light, I give every person who seeks Light the opportunity to heal through compassion and empathy, enabling them to begin to release their pain.

I encourage people to recognise and exercise free will, which helps them make empowered and better decisions.

As a facilitator of Light, I also must accept the free will choices of my client.

Self-healing works through Light awareness. The sense of Light I attune to intuits feelings of wholeness that permit me to see what requires healing within my mind. This sense of Light shines its brightness into the darkness of my mind to help me heal and release my barriers of pain.

When I apply any one of the sensory boundaries of Light awareness, I protect my vibrations of Light.

When I apply any one of Light's sensory boundaries, I provide myself with that space to not react to my bravado perspective and the automatic demands it makes of me.

Self-healing works for me through my Light awareness building, which happens as I seek and connect to Light during my work, or as I sleep, when I meditate or when I consciously observe humanity and nature.

Observing my thoughts, interactions with others and interactions within my mind and behaviour will always be essential.

Taking and accepting responsibility for myself, the person, for all the emotions and spirit entities I had permitted to cling to me continues to be the essential drive for my evolving self-healing.

I began self-healing without drama, silently within me at my core existence of Light.

Self-healing is a life journey that ensures a person makes changes that are for life.

Self-healing facilitates the cultivation of a Light awareness and its truth interpreted by the higher self, the Light within.

I accepted that I needed to cultivate an inner discipline that enabled me to hold my Light vibration to uphold Light awareness.

Several more meditations to those listed can take you into the depths of your irrational thoughts, irrational emotions, and the spiritual and religious teachings that may have crippled and frozen your feelings and emotions in pain.

These meditations will empower your self-healing intention into a further impetus for advancement in your evolution. However, to experience these meditations so that you are entirely mentally safe and protected, I must help you engage with your Light awareness that ensures you do not regress to your learning when you endeavour to depower your pain.

Insights that help reveal the invisible mental barriers

What is Anxiety?

I believe anxiety happens when the inner mind floods with unknown, invisible emotions of irrational fears or anger that override a person's voice in their usual mindset. It manifests as an invisible out-of-control dread of paralysis within the mind that the person cannot control. Why?

It is a learned way of coping for a person's mind that has developed automatically with challenges they have had to face and automatically think they cannot do, cope with, or face. For example, a child goes to school, which the child doesn't want to do. Or a person who feels overwhelmed and paralysed by work pressure and can no longer face work because of the fear of exposure and failure.

The invisible physical actions of fear can vary for people. Still, the most common actions felt in the body are as follows: the fear of other people's anger, the fear of not being liked, and the fear of isolation from family, friends, or peers. The invisible hand as it clutches the body, especially the throat, resulting in choking sensations. Or the chest area is overcome by a force of energy, resulting in an inability to breathe. Or the fear of a physical heart attack resulting in death. Anxiety can also manifest in irritable bowel symptoms or severe constipation. It can also manifest in the physical heart with sensations of fluttering.

Yet, mostly these attacks are experienced as the person is lying safely in bed or sitting at home feeling paralysed internally in their mind, unable to help themselves until the paralysis fades.

I understand anxiety begins with an automatic single adrenaline-fuelled fear, mainly of failure in the eyes of the family. It can begin with the challenge of going to school for a child. The child may be frightened of a teacher that it cannot articulate and does not want to meet the teacher. The child has no control and must obey the adults. The fear builds daily in the child's mind, and each new fear kicks into the invisible automatic fear that can sometimes overwhelm a child. The fear becomes a worry or automatic anger, forming the basics of a child's mindset. It can be seen in their worried facial expressions. It will eventually manifest in the child/adult's mind as an overwhelming fear or anger that triggers their irrational behaviour. Or the child/adult can grow to become isolated and introverted in its mindset. The anxiety continues because the child/adult feels they do not have a choice, ability, or right to say no. It becomes a self-created invisible weapon of the mind fuelling the release of massive amounts of adrenaline that works against a person's mind and physical body. Anxiety can manifest in the adult as a fear of going to work and facing work colleagues and is recognisable in most relationships, mainly between boss and adult or husband and wife or parent and child.

As I write out these symptoms, they can develop into many physical diseases in the body and mind.

When a person reaches the investigative stage of their anxiety, it means the anxiety is in control of the mind. Usually, they find themselves in a doctor's surgery, advised to take medication to control it.

I believe anxiety can be self-healed one thought at a time and by the discipline of detachment through a Light perspective and Light awareness. There is no anxiety, fear or anger in Light awareness.

The Second Meditation

An Introduction to Light and the realignment of the upper spiritual chakras into Light existence.

The second meditation we are about to begin is an introduction to the Light within. In this meditation, you attune the senses to reveal the upper chakra system and realign it to the Light. Again, if your mantra breathing is not a confident, practised technique for you, there is no point in doing the following meditation. Please go back and practice your mantra technique.

The spiritual chakras are the heart, throat, third eye and crown chakras, when realigned in Light, make up the imprint of your Light within.

To feel better in your heart and body, practice this meditation daily.

It is essential to take exact steps that repeat and repeat throughout the meditation to help you build confidence in attuning to Light, the aura and chakras,

It takes considerable trust and belief in one's intention to connect to Light as we approach Light from an intuitive awareness of darkness.

Each step we take into the awareness of Light is the most challenging for the mind to accept.

Your thoughts will diminish the meditation by drawing you back to the bravado's thoughts of security, comfort and learning. You must know you are determined to find and connect to Light, the higher self.

To start your meditation, find a room you will not be disturbed to use for about one hour. Place a candle on a table before you and light it; dedicate your intention to reach and connect to Light. For the best results from the meditation, it is best to sit on a chair. Place the feet firmly on the ground. The small of the back pushed into the support of the chair. Loosely fold your hands on your lap. All your breathing must inhale through the nose and exhale through the mouth. Start this meditation by doing your mantra breathing for fifteen in-breaths. As the mantra takes effect in your senses, you will feel the tension melting away from your body, and you will feel ready to begin to seek the Light within.

Open and focus the eyes and the senses on the
candle flame to reconnect your senses to Light.

Continue to breathe in light for five in-breaths. Consciously slow down the breathing by counting to five as you breathe in, counting to five as you hold your breath, and counting to five as you exhale through the mouth.

> Slowly breathe in light for a count of five. Hold it in your lungs for a count of five. Breathe out light for a count of five as you exhale through the mouth.

Slowly breathe in light for a count of five. Hold it in your lungs for a count of five. Breathe out light for a count of five as you exhale through the mouth.

Slowly breathe in light for a count of five. Hold it in your lungs for a count of five. Breathe out light for a count of five as you exhale through the mouth.

Slowly breathe in light for a count of five. Hold it in your lungs for a count of five. Breathe out light for a count of five as you exhale through the mouth.

Slowly breathe in light for a count of five. Hold it in your lungs for a count of five. Breathe out light for a count of five as you exhale through the mouth.

Close your eyes. Continue breathing in the rhythm of the mantra breathing.

Roll the eyes inwards towards the bridge of the nose area. You are looking for a reflected candle flame that may appear in your third eye space. With the eyes closed, continue to breathe, and say the mantra for three in-breaths.

Slowly breathe light up through the nose to reach the internal flame in your third eye chakra. Hold your breath in your lungs. Focus the light from the third eye chakra downwards to connect to the light in the heart chakra. Slowly exhale light through the mouth for a count of five.

Next, slowly breathe light up through the nose to reach the internal flame in your third eye chakra. Hold your breath in your lungs. Focus the light from the third eye chakra downwards to connect to the light in the heart chakra. Slowly exhale light through the mouth for a count of five.

Again, slowly breathe light up through the nose to reach the internal flame in your third eye chakra. Hold your breath in your lungs. Focus the light from the third eye chakra downwards to connect to the light in the heart chakra. Slowly exhale light through the mouth for a count of five.

Keep your eyes closed and repeat.

Slowly breathe light up through the nose to reach the internal flame in your third eye chakra. Hold your breath in your lungs. Focus the light from the third eye chakra downwards to connect to the light in the heart chakra. Slowly exhale light through the mouth for a count of five.

Next, slowly breathe light up through the nose to reach the internal flame in your third eye chakra. Hold your breath in your lungs. Focus the light from the third eye chakra downwards to connect to the light in the heart chakra. Slowly exhale light through the mouth for a count of five.

Again, slowly breathe light up through the nose to reach the internal flame in your third eye chakra. Hold your breath in your lungs. Focus the light from the third eye chakra downwards to connect to the light in the heart chakra. Slowly exhale light through the mouth for a count of five.

Keep your eyes closed and repeat.

Slowly breathe light up through the nose to reach the internal flame in your third eye chakra. Hold your breath in your lungs. Focus the light from the third eye chakra downwards to connect to the light in the heart chakra. Slowly exhale light through the mouth for a count of five.

Next, slowly breathe light up through the nose to reach the internal flame in your third eye chakra. Hold your breath in your lungs. Focus the light from the third eye chakra downwards to connect to the light in the heart chakra. Slowly exhale light through the mouth for a count of five.

Again, slowly breathe light up through the nose to reach the internal flame in your third eye chakra. Hold your breath in your lungs. Focus the light from the third eye chakra downwards to connect to the light in the heart chakra. Slowly exhale light through the mouth for a count of five.

Let us begin our meditation

1. Crown Chakra

Draw the senses inwards by closing the eyes. Slowly breathe light up through the nose to reach the internal flame in your third eye chakra. Next, hold your breath in your lungs as you focus the light from the third eye chakra upwards to exit through the crown chakra to seek and connect to the highest vibration of the Light of the universe. As you slowly exhale, ask the highest Light to awaken your sensory body into the awareness of the highest Light vibrations.

Open your eyes. Focus your senses outwards to the candle flame. Commence the mantra breathing for three in-breaths to reconnect your senses to Light.

Draw the senses inwards by closing the eyes. Slowly breathe light up through the nose to reach the internal flame in your third eye chakra. Next, hold your breath in your lungs as you focus the light from the third eye chakra upwards to exit through the crown chakra to seek and connect to the highest vibration of the Light of the universe. As you slowly exhale, ask the highest Light to connect and ignite your senses into the reality of the highest Light vibrations.

Open your eyes. Focus your senses outwards to the candle flame. Commence the mantra breathing for three in-breaths to reconnect your senses to Light.

Draw the senses inwards by closing the eyes. Slowly breathe light up through the nose to reach the internal flame in your third eye chakra. Next, hold your breath in your lungs as you focus the light from the third eye chakra upwards to exit through the crown chakra to seek and connect to the highest vibration of the Light of the universe. As you slowly exhale, ask the highest Light to awaken the Light in the crown chakra to enable it to connect to the highest Light vibration for support and influence.

Open your eyes. Focus your senses outwards to the candle flame. Commence the mantra breathing for three in-breaths to reconnect your senses to Light.

Draw the senses inwards by closing the eyes. Slowly breathe light up through the nose to reach the internal flame in your third eye chakra. Next, hold your breath in your lungs as you focus the light from the third eye chakra upwards to exit through the crown chakra to seek and connect to the highest vibration of the Light of the universe. As you slowly exhale, ask the highest Light to ignite and spin the crown chakra existence into the intention of the highest Light vibrations while realigning it to its correct position on the top of the head.

Open your eyes. Focus your senses outwards to the candle flame. Commence the mantra breathing for three in-breaths to reconnect your senses to Light.

2. Third Eye Chakra

Draw the senses inwards by closing your eyes. Slowly breathe light up through your nose to reach the internal flame in your third eye chakra. Hold your breath in your lungs as you focus the light from the third eye chakra upwards to exit through the crown chakra to seek and connect to the highest vibration of the Light of the universe. As you slowly exhale, ask the highest Light to awaken your sensory body into the awareness of the highest Light vibrations.

Open your eyes. Focus your senses outwards to the candle flame. Commence the mantra breathing for three in-breaths to reconnect your senses to Light.

Draw the senses inwards by closing your eyes. Slowly breathe light up through your nose to reach the internal flame in your third eye chakra. Hold your breath in your lungs as you focus the light from the third eye chakra upwards to exit through the crown chakra to seek and connect to the highest vibration of the Light of the universe.

As you slowly exhale, ask the highest Light to connect and ignite your senses into the reality of the highest Light vibrations.

Open your eyes. Focus your senses outwards to the candle flame. Commence the mantra breathing for three in-breaths to reconnect your senses to Light.

Draw the senses inwards by closing your eyes. Slowly breathe light up through your nose to reach the internal flame in your third eye chakra. Hold your breath in your lungs as you focus the light from the third eye chakra upwards to exit through the crown chakra to seek and connect to the highest vibration of the Light of the universe. As you slowly exhale, ask the highest Light to awaken the Light in the third eye chakra to enable it to connect to the highest Light vibration for support and influence.

Open your eyes. Focus your senses outwards to the candle flame. Commence the mantra breathing for three in-breaths to reconnect your senses to Light.

Draw the senses inwards by closing your eyes. Slowly breathe light up through your nose to reach the internal flame in your third eye chakra. Hold your breath in your lungs as you focus the light from the third eye chakra upwards to exit through the crown chakra to seek and connect to the highest vibration of the Light of the universe. As you slowly exhale, ask the highest Light to ignite and spin the third eye chakra existence into the intention of the highest Light vibrations while realigning it to its correct position in the centre of the forehead.

Open your eyes. Focus your senses outwards to the candle flame. Commence the mantra breathing for three in-breaths to reconnect your senses to Light.

3. Throat Chakra

Draw the senses inwards by closing the eyes. Slowly breathe light up through your nose to reach the internal flame in your third eye chakra. Hold your breath in your lungs as you focus the light from the third eye chakra upwards to exit through the crown chakra to seek and connect to the highest vibration of the Light of the universe. As you slowly exhale, ask the highest Light to awaken your sensory body into the highest Light vibrations.

Open your eyes. Focus your senses outwards to the candle flame. Commence the mantra breathing for three in-breaths to reconnect your senses to Light.

Draw the senses inwards by closing the eyes. Slowly breathe light up through your nose to reach the internal flame in your third eye chakra. Hold your breath in your lungs as you focus the light from the third eye chakra upwards to exit through the crown chakra to seek and connect to the highest vibration of the Light of the universe.

As you slowly exhale, ask the highest Light to connect and ignite your senses into the reality of the highest Light vibrations.

Open your eyes. Focus your senses outwards to the candle flame. Commence the mantra breathing for three in-breaths to reconnect your senses to Light.

Draw the senses inwards by closing the eyes. Slowly breathe light up through your nose to reach the internal flame in your third eye chakra. Hold your breath in your lungs as you focus the light from the third eye chakra upwards to exit through the crown chakra to seek and connect to the highest vibration of the Light of the universe. As you slowly exhale, ask the highest Light to awaken the Light in the throat chakra to enable it to connect to the highest Light vibration for support and influence.

Open your eyes. Focus your senses outwards to the candle flame. Commence the mantra breathing for three in-breaths to reconnect your senses to Light.

Draw the senses inwards by closing the eyes. Slowly breathe light up through your nose to reach the internal flame in your third eye chakra. Hold your breath in your lungs as you focus the light from the third eye chakra upwards to exit through the crown chakra to seek and connect to the highest vibration of the Light of the universe. As you slowly exhale, ask the highest Light to ignite and spin the throat chakra existence into the intention of the highest Light vibrations while realigning it to its correct position in the centre of the throat and neck.

Open your eyes. Focus your senses outwards to the candle flame. Commence the mantra breathing for three in-breaths to reconnect your senses to Light.

4. Heart Chakra

Draw the senses inwards by closing the eyes. Slowly breathe light up through your nose to reach the internal flame in your third eye chakra. Hold your breath in your lungs as you focus the light from the third eye chakra upwards to exit through the crown chakra to seek and connect to the highest vibration of the Light of the universe. As you slowly exhale, ask the highest Light to awaken your sensory body into the awareness of the highest Light vibrations.

Open your eyes. Focus your senses outwards to the candle flame. Commence the mantra breathing for three in-breaths to reconnect your senses to Light.

Draw the senses inwards by closing the eyes. Slowly breathe light up through your nose to reach the internal flame in your third eye chakra. Hold your breath in your lungs as you focus the light from the third eye chakra upwards to exit through the crown chakra to seek and connect to the highest vibration of the Light of the universe. As you slowly exhale, ask the highest Light to connect and ignite your senses into the reality of the highest Light vibrations.

Open your eyes. Focus your senses outwards to the candle flame. Commence the mantra breathing for three in-breaths to reconnect your senses to Light.

Draw the senses inwards by closing the eyes. Slowly breathe light up through your nose to reach the internal flame in your third eye chakra. Hold your breath in your lungs as you focus the light from the third eye chakra upwards to exit through the crown chakra to seek and connect to the highest vibration of the Light of the universe. As you slowly exhale, ask the highest Light to awaken the Light in the heart chakra to enable it to connect to the highest Light vibration for support and influence.

Open your eyes. Focus your senses outwards to the candle flame. Commence the mantra breathing for three in-breaths to reconnect your senses to Light.

Draw the senses inwards by closing the eyes. Slowly breathe light up through your nose to reach the internal flame in your third eye chakra. Hold your breath in your lungs as you focus the light from the third eye chakra upwards to exit through the crown chakra to seek and connect to the highest vibration of the Light of the universe.

As you slowly exhale, ask the highest Light to ignite and spin the heart chakra existence into the intention of the highest Light vibrations while realigning it to its correct position in the centre of the chest in the breastbone.

Open your eyes. Focus your senses outwards to the candle flame. Commence the mantra breathing for three in-breaths to reconnect your senses to Light.

Draw the senses inwards by closing the eyes. Slowly breathe light up through your nose to reach the internal flame in your third eye chakra. Hold your breath in your lungs as you focus the light from the third eye chakra upwards to exit through the crown chakra to seek and connect to the highest vibration of the Light of the universe. As you slowly exhale, invite the highest Light to connect to the unique Light within the heart chakra to support and strengthen It whilst you meditate.

Open your eyes. Focus your senses outwards to the candle flame. Commence the mantra breathing for three in-breaths to reconnect your senses to Light.

As you gaze at the candle flame, welcome the Light from the highest vibration into your heart and ask for Its support as you meditate.

Close your eyes and refocus your senses to the regular mantra breathing.

Remember, you have realigned and ignited your spiritual chakras into a reflection of the brilliance of the highest Light of the universe.

Feel the vibrancy of this Light within you.

If thoughts intrude into your meditation, please instantly revert to the mantra breathing and breath them out as you exhale.

Remember, you are sitting in a sacred, protected space of Light.

You need to sense and feel Light.

After twenty in-breaths, or ten minutes which you can extend as you gain confidence in your meditating skills, draw your awareness back to the Light of the heart chakra and thank Light from the highest vibration for visiting you. It is essential to deliberately RELEASE this Light back upwards to the highest Light of the universe as you close your meditation.

Before you open your eyes and become physical again, it is essential to ground your aligned chakras into your consciousness.

Grounding

Begin by placing your hand on your head and imagining your hand is a beacon of bright shining Light. Imagine you are directing its Light downwards through the realigned internal chakra system. The Light enters the ground by exiting through the feet chakras, delving deep into the earth's energies to develop massive tree-like roots helping you to remain in a Light awareness until next time.

Insights that help build your Light Awareness

Meditation Experiences

While you meditate and breathe the mantra, ask Light some questions.

For example, please help me to sense the Light in the room.

Do not expect to receive instant answers to your questions, but answers may manifest in future meditations.

If your mind is troublesome, revert to mantra breathing and sense the Light of the mantra.

Do not seek your mind's familiar learning or comfort zones of deity during your meditation.

Challenge yourself to interpret the highest vibration of Light for your wisdom. Accept this wisdom

Sometimes, your Light awareness travels a universal journey to explore the sensations of the universe during this meditation.

When this happens, observe if fear kicks into your lower chakras. The fear in your mind or the unconscious fear of the spirit may intrude on your Light space. When this happens, stay detached entirely from the intrusions by refocusing your senses on your mantra breathing. It is important to recall your fear and how it felt to you.

The mind will tell you that seeking Light is dull; the meditation is too long and repetitive, and your frustrations can take over.

Please recognise that these are your learned thoughts that want to hold you in their control.

Ask Light for help and courage.

Do not give your mind power in this meditation. If you do, you will find yourself spinning in your learning which is full of bravado.

The sensations of the Light felt during this meditation can be profound.

Insights that help build your Light Awareness

The Subtle Reveal of Light

The Light within meditation facilitates each person to reveal their Light, aura, chakra system, and senses.

From this Light perspective, I changed myself, changed my mindset and healed myself.

From this Light perspective, I understood and accepted that I needed to seek Light through my senses.

When I sought Light from a learned perspective, consciously, subconsciously, or unconsciously, I connected to God automatically through my religious or spiritual influences.

From a Light perspective, I began to accept that spirit and religion reflect the learned conditioned collective mindset of humanity, which means there is little difference between the vibration of the known conditioned collective mind of the human and the invisible spirit and religion dynamics.

Prayers for healing and Light Awareness

Light, please help me to trust my senses and my intuition.

Light, please give me the courage to detach from my learning.

Please help me let go of the comfort zones of my learned conditioned love.

Please help me let go of the familiar unthinking thinking of my automatic mindset.

I pray for truth and ask Light to find the inner strength to accept the truth.

Insights that help build your Light Awareness

Happiness and Peace

I understand that if I can ever feel true happiness and peace, I must respect and honour the feelings of Light awareness.

I need my senses to vibrate at a very high Light vibration to achieve clarity and vision.

I must work only with the highest Light vibration to achieve these standards.

Prayers for healing and Light Awareness

I pray to Light to help me sense and accept Light within me.

I pray to Light to help me withstand my conditioned mind's pressures that pull me into the familiar and learned, unthinking automatic ways of my mind.

I pray for dignity as I ask Light to please show me dignity because I do not know how dignity feels in my awareness.

Insights that help build your Light Awareness

Grounding

It becomes easy to forget to ground oneself in Light because of the automatically learned perception and perspective of power.

If you become conscious of the spinning in your thoughts and think you have reached your breaking point, or feel attacked psychically, take a step back mentally and do the following grounding exercise.

You will instantly feel better.

Begin by placing your hand on top of your head and imagine your hand is a beacon of bright shining Light. Imagine you are directing its Light downwards through the internal chakra system. The Light enters the ground by exiting through the feet chakras, delving deep into the earth's energies to develop massive tree-like roots helping you to remain in a Light awareness and focused on Light's strength.

Light awareness detaches you from the emotions that may affect you, whether yours or someone else's.

Please take a moment to settle into Light sensations.

Prayers for healing and Light Awareness

Light, please help me feel the inner strength of my heart chakra.

Insights that help recognise your mental barriers

To Feel

Every sensation is an opportunity to feel.
Every feeling is an opportunity to evolve.
Every idea is an opportunity to release.
All emotion is an opportunity to transmute
pain into Light.

Prayers for healing and Light Awareness

Light, please give me the courage to trust my feelings.

Light, please give me the courage to begin to heal my emotions.

Light, please give me the courage not to remain in a fearful state because I am too frightened to face my emotions.

Please give me the courage to face my pain and not be frightened.

Light, please help me to step into my pain and not to be afraid of it.

Please help me release pain by trusting myself, the Light within.

Insights that help you recognise your mental barriers

Denial

Denial is a powerful mind barrier that prevents you from taking full responsibility for your thoughts and actions. It is an automatic mechanism that influences the mind in shadowed irresponsible and childlike behaviour.

Avoidance is another aspect of denial.

Absenteeism is another aspect of denial.

Guilt is another emotion of negative passivity that permits unacceptable behaviour to infiltrate feelings, hence maintaining pain levels.

Do not deny yourself the opportunity to connect to your Light, your higher self.

Consciously develop a disciplined boundary to help you nurture your higher ideals.

Prayers for healing and Light Awareness

Light, please help me to sense and feel Light.

Please help me detach from my anger and my dismissive behaviour.

Light, please help me to find my denial and my irresponsible thinking and behaviour.

Please, Light, show me guilt so I can recognise my mind's stagnation by guilt.

I need to identify guilt in all its invisible shapes.

Insights that help reveal the invisible mental barriers

Ignorance

In my bravado mind, I assumed the ignorance I identified in other people was the instant response or the momentary reaction to an opinion or behaviour.

Now through my Light awareness, ignorance is a mindset.

When I accepted this insight, I felt better about my relationships, especially those I needed to break away from because I could not negotiate a better relationship.

Ignorance is a controlling, authoritarian mindset that is right in its opinion and control.

Seek the courage to ask yourself if your mindset is ignorant.

Insights that help build your Light Awareness

Acceptance

Acceptance is a fantastic unconditional gift of love from God. It permits you to accept the Light influences without needing a physical shape or any outside interference to come between you and your higher self which is Light.

When you accept that Light's sensations are real, you will find the courage to let go of the automatic want to feel conditional love.

Learning is the most potent but lethal weapon of the mind.

Learning is mostly about what you perceive or interpret, or it is taught to you from a very young, innocent age by others.

Yet your learning is not you. It is not your true identity.

Prayers for healing and Light Awareness

I pray to Light for a sense of acceptance, so I know how acceptance feels.

I pray to Light to help me to feel unconditional love and to accept its existence within my heart.

I pray to Light to inspire me to build my unique boundaries.

I pray for Light's courage to help me to seek and reveal the truth of Light, my truth and the shadowed truth of the learned mind.

I pray to Light for Its compassion and empathy to help me accept my sensory pain and give me the courage to deal with it.

I pray to Light to give me the courage to let go of my learning and find acceptance in my awareness of my insights and inspirations.

It is best to use one prayer each time you meditate, as it is easier to sense or interpret the single answer required from Light.

Insights that help build your Light Awareness

Observance

To help your Light perspective, it is essential to consciously build your observance tool in Light awareness and not from your learned perspective.

The observance of your inner mind especially can be difficult. Light will permit you to see it without judgement. When you observe your thoughts in meditation, are you recognising any negative traits? For example, can you see if you resist meditation by engaging in familiar negative thoughts?

Can you see if your thoughts are impatient or angry? Consider recognising this impatience and anger by identifying how you interact in your relationships.

You must observe your thoughts outside of meditation and watch your actions and reactions as you feel challenged in different relationships and situations.

Prayers for healing and Light Awareness

I pray to Light to help me recognise my judgments and help me detach and release this mechanism in my mind.

I pray to Light to help me feel compassion for myself as I begin to see who I am in my mind.

I pray to Light to help me to accept my thought dynamic and to detach from its process.

I pray to Light to show me the courage and help me accept clarity in my awareness.

The following meditation is the longest so far. It takes time and patience.

If you feel you cannot give it time or patience, focus the meditation on one chakra at a time or continue practising the upper chakras realignment meditation until you are fully confident of your meditation.

You will naturally advance to the next stage of meditation.

The Third Meditation

A n Introduction to Light and the Realignment of the Whole Chakra System to a Light Existence

Practice this meditation daily.

The whole chakra system comprises the upper chakras, the heart, throat, third eye, crown chakras and the lower chakras, the solar plexus, sacral, base and feet chakras.

It is essential to take exact steps that repeat and repeat throughout the meditation, which will help you build confidence in attuning to Light, the aura and chakras.

It takes considerable trust and belief in one's intention to connect to Light as we approach Light from an awareness of darkness.

Each step we take into the awareness of Light is the most challenging for the mind to accept.

Your thoughts will diminish the meditation by drawing you back to the bravado's thoughts of security, comfort and learning. You must know you are determined to find and connect to Light, the higher self.

To start your meditation, find a room you will not be disturbed in to use for about one hour. Place a candle on a table before you and light it. As you light it, dedicate your intention to reach and connect to Light. For best results from the meditation, it is best to sit on a chair. Place the feet firmly on the ground, the small of the back pushed into the support of the chair. Loosely fold your hands on your lap. All your breathing must inhale through the nose and exhale through the mouth. Start this meditation by doing your mantra breathing for fifteen in-breaths. As the mantra takes effect in your senses, you will feel the tension melting away from your body, and you will feel ready to begin to seek the Light within.

Open your eyes. Focus your senses outwards to the candle flame. Commence the mantra breathing for five in-breaths to reconnect your senses to Light.

Consciously slow down the breathing by counting to five as you breathe in, counting to five as you hold your breath, and counting to five as you exhale through the mouth.

Slowly breathe in light for a count of five, hold it in your lungs for a count of five/breathe out light for a count of five as you exhale through the mouth.

Slowly breathe in light for a count of five, hold it in your lungs for a count of five/breathe out light for a count of five as you exhale through the mouth.

Slowly breathe in light for a count of five, hold it in your lungs for a count of five/breathe out light for a count of five as you exhale through the mouth.

Slowly breathe in light for a count of five, hold it in your lungs for a count of five/breathe out light for a count of five as you exhale through the mouth.

Slowly breathe in light for a count of five, hold it in your lungs for a count of five/breathe out light for a count of five as you exhale through the mouth.

Close your eyes. Continue breathing in the rhythm of the mantra breathing.

Roll the eyes inwards towards the bridge of the nose area. You are looking for a reflected candle flame that may appear in your third eye space. With the eyes closed, continue to breathe, and say the mantra for three in-breaths.

Slowly breathe light up through the nose to reach the internal flame in your third eye chakra. Hold your breath in your lungs. Focus the light from the third eye chakra downwards to connect to the light in the heart chakra. Slowly exhale light through the mouth for a count of five.

Next, slowly breathe light up through the nose to reach the internal flame in your third eye chakra. Hold your breath in your lungs. Focus the light from the third eye chakra downwards to connect to the light in the heart chakra. Slowly exhale light through the mouth for a count of five.

Again, slowly breathe light up through the nose to reach the internal flame in your third eye chakra. Hold your breath in your lungs. Focus the light from the third eye chakra downwards to connect to the light in the heart

chakra. Slowly exhale light through the mouth for a count of five.

Keep your eyes closed and repeat.

Slowly breathe light up through the nose to reach the internal flame in your third eye chakra. Hold your breath in your lungs. Focus the light from the third eye chakra downwards to connect to the light in the heart chakra. Slowly exhale light through the mouth for a count of five.

Next, slowly breathe light up through the nose to reach the internal flame in your third eye chakra. Hold your breath in your lungs. Focus the light from the third eye chakra downwards to connect to the light in the heart chakra. Slowly exhale light through the mouth for a count of five.

Again, slowly breathe light up through the nose to reach the internal flame in your third eye chakra. Hold your breath in your lungs. Focus the light from the third eye chakra downwards to connect to the light in the heart chakra. Slowly exhale light through the mouth for a count of five.

Let us begin our meditation.

1. Crown Chakra

Draw the senses inwards by closing the eyes. Slowly breathe light up through your nose to reach the internal flame in your third eye chakra. Hold your breath in your

lungs as you focus the light from the third eye chakra upwards to exit through the crown chakra to seek and connect to the highest vibration of the Light of the universe. As you slowly exhale, ask the highest Light to awaken your sensory body into the awareness of the highest Light vibrations.

Open your eyes. Focus your senses outwards to the candle flame. Commence the mantra breathing for three in-breaths to reconnect your senses to Light.

Draw the senses inwards by closing the eyes. Slowly breathe light up through your nose to reach the internal flame in your third eye chakra. Hold your breath in your lungs as you focus the light from the third eye chakra upwards to exit through the crown chakra to seek and connect to the highest vibration of the Light of the universe. As you slowly exhale, ask the highest Light to connect and ignite your senses into the reality of the highest Light vibrations.

Open your eyes. Focus your senses outwards to the candle flame. Commence the mantra breathing for three in-breaths to reconnect your senses to Light.

Draw the senses inwards by closing the eyes. Slowly breathe light up through your nose to reach the internal flame in your third eye chakra. Hold your breath in your lungs as you focus the light from the third eye chakra upwards to exit through the crown chakra to seek and connect to the highest vibration of the Light of the universe. As you slowly exhale, ask the highest Light to awaken the Light in the crown chakra to enable it to connect to the highest Light vibration for support and influence.

Open your eyes. Focus your senses outwards to the candle flame. Commence the mantra breathing for three in-breaths to reconnect your senses to Light.

Draw the senses inwards by closing the eyes. Slowly breathe light up through your nose to reach the internal flame in your third eye chakra. Hold your breath in your lungs as you focus the light from the third eye chakra upwards to exit through the crown chakra to seek and connect to the highest vibration of the Light of the universe. As you slowly exhale, ask the highest Light to ignite and spin the crown chakra existence into the intention of the highest Light vibrations while realigning it to its correct position on the top of the head.

Open your eyes. Focus your senses outwards to the candle flame. Commence the mantra breathing for three in-breaths to reconnect your senses to Light.

2. Third Eye Chakra

Draw the senses inwards by closing the eyes. Slowly breathe light up through your nose to reach the internal

flame in your third eye chakra. Hold your breath in your lungs as you focus the light from the third eye chakra upwards to exit through the crown chakra to seek and connect to the highest vibration of the Light of the universe. As you slowly exhale, ask the highest Light to awaken your sensory body into the awareness of the highest Light vibrations.

Open your eyes. Focus your senses outwards to the candle flame. Commence the mantra breathing for three in-breaths to reconnect your senses to Light.

Draw the senses inwards by closing the eyes. Slowly breathe light up through your nose to reach the internal flame in your third eye chakra. Hold your breath in your lungs as you focus the light from the third eye chakra upwards to exit through the crown chakra to seek and connect to the highest vibration of the Light of the universe. As you slowly exhale, ask the highest Light to connect and ignite your senses into the reality of the highest Light vibrations.

Open your eyes. Focus your senses outwards to the candle flame. Commence the mantra breathing for three in-breaths to reconnect your senses to Light.

Draw the senses inwards by closing the eyes. Slowly breathe light up through your nose to reach the internal flame in your third eye chakra. Hold your breath in your

lungs as you focus the light from the third eye chakra upwards to exit through the crown chakra to seek and connect to the highest vibration of the Light of the universe. As you slowly exhale, ask the highest Light to awaken the Light in the third eye chakra to enable it to connect to the highest Light vibration for support and influence.

Open your eyes. Focus your senses outwards to the candle flame. Commence the mantra breathing for three in-breaths to reconnect your senses to Light.

Draw the senses inwards by closing the eyes Slowly breathe light up through your nose to reach the internal flame in your third eye chakra. Hold your breath in your lungs as you focus the light from the third eye chakra upwards to exit through the crown chakra to seek and connect to the highest vibration of the Light of the universe. As you slowly exhale, ask the highest Light to ignite and spin the third eye chakra existence into the intention of the highest Light vibrations while realigning it to its correct position in the centre of the forehead.

Open your eyes. Focus your senses outwards to the candle flame. Commence the mantra breathing for three in-breaths to reconnect your senses to Light.

3. Throat Chakra

Draw the senses inwards by closing the eyes. Slowly breathe light up through your nose to reach the internal flame in your third eye chakra. Hold your breath in your lungs as you focus the light from the third eye chakra upwards to exit through the crown chakra to seek and connect to the highest vibration of the Light of the universe. As you slowly exhale, ask the highest Light to awaken your sensory body into the awareness of the highest Light vibrations.

Open your eyes. Focus your senses outwards to the candle flame. Commence the mantra breathing for three in-breaths to reconnect your senses to Light.

Draw the senses inwards by closing the eyes. Slowly breathe light up through your nose to reach the internal flame in your third eye chakra. Hold your breath in your lungs as you focus the light from the third eye chakra upwards to exit through the crown chakra to seek and connect to the highest vibration of the Light of the universe. As you slowly exhale, ask the highest Light to connect and ignite your senses into the reality of the highest Light vibrations.

Open your eyes. Focus your senses outwards to the candle flame. Commence the mantra breathing for three in-breaths to reconnect your senses to Light.

Draw the senses inwards by closing the eyes. Slowly breathe light up through your nose to reach the internal flame in your third eye chakra. Hold your breath in your lungs as you focus the light from the third eye chakra upwards to exit through the crown chakra to seek and connect to the highest vibration of the Light of the universe. As you slowly exhale, ask the highest Light to awaken the Light in the throat chakra to enable it to connect to the highest Light vibration for support and influence.

Open your eyes. Focus your senses outwards to the candle flame. Commence the mantra breathing for three in-breaths to reconnect your senses to Light.

Draw the senses inwards by closing the eyes. Slowly breathe light up through your nose to reach the internal flame in your third eye chakra. Hold your breath in your lungs as you focus the light from the third eye chakra upwards to exit through the crown chakra to seek and connect to the highest vibration of the Light of the universe. As you slowly exhale, ask the highest Light to ignite and spin the throat chakra existence into the intention of the highest Light vibrations while realigning it to its correct position in the centre of the throat and neck.

Open your eyes. Focus your senses outwards to the candle flame. Commence the mantra breathing for three in-breaths to reconnect your senses to Light.

4. Heart Chakra

Draw the senses inwards by closing the eyes. Slowly breathe light up through your nose to reach the internal flame in your third eye chakra. Hold your breath in your lungs as you focus the light from the third eye chakra upwards to exit through the crown chakra to seek and connect to the highest vibration of the Light of the universe. As you slowly exhale, ask the highest Light to awaken your sensory body into the awareness of the highest Light vibrations.

Open your eyes. Focus your senses outwards to the candle flame. Commence the mantra breathing for three in-breaths to reconnect your senses to Light.

Draw the senses inwards by closing the eyes. Slowly breathe light up through your nose to reach the internal flame in your third eye chakra. Hold your breath in your lungs as you focus the light from the third eye chakra upwards to exit through the crown chakra to seek and connect to the highest vibration of the Light of the universe. As you slowly exhale, ask the highest Light to connect and ignite your senses into the reality of the highest Light vibrations.

Open your eyes. Focus your senses outwards to the candle flame. Commence the mantra breathing for three in-breaths to reconnect your senses to Light.

Draw the senses inwards by closing the eyes. Slowly breathe light up through your nose to reach the internal flame in your third eye chakra. Hold your breath in your lungs as you focus the light from the third eye chakra upwards to exit through the crown chakra to seek and connect to the highest vibration of the Light of the universe. As you slowly exhale, ask the highest Light to awaken the Light in the heart chakra to enable it to connect to the highest Light vibration for support and influence.

Open your eyes. Focus your senses outwards to the candle flame. Commence the mantra breathing for three in-breaths to reconnect your senses to Light.

Draw the senses inwards by closing the eyes. Slowly breathe light up through your nose to reach the internal flame in your third eye chakra. Hold your breath in your lungs as you focus the light from the third eye chakra upwards to exit through the crown chakra to seek and connect to the highest vibration of the Light of the universe. As you slowly exhale, ask the highest Light to ignite and spin the heart chakra existence into the intention of the highest Light vibrations while realigning it to its correct position in the centre of the chest in the breastbone.

Open your eyes. Focus your senses outwards to the candle flame. Commence the mantra breathing for three in-breaths to reconnect your senses to Light.

Draw the senses inwards by closing the eyes. Slowly breathe light up through your nose to reach the internal flame in your third eye chakra. Hold your breath in your lungs as you focus the light from the third eye chakra upwards to exit through the crown chakra to seek and connect to the highest vibration of the Light of the universe. As you slowly exhale, invite the highest Light to connect to the unique Light within the heart chakra to support and strengthen It whilst you meditate.

Open your eyes. Focus your senses outwards to the candle flame. Commence the mantra breathing for three in-breaths to reconnect your senses to Light.

As you gaze at the candle flame, welcome the Light from the highest vibration into your heart and ask for Its support as you meditate.

5. Solar Plexus Chakra

Draw the senses inwards by closing the eyes. Slowly breathe light up through your nose to reach the internal flame in your third eye chakra. Hold your breath in your lungs as you focus the light from the third eye chakra upwards to exit through the crown chakra to seek and connect to the highest vibration of the Light of the universe. As you slowly exhale, ask the highest Light to awaken your sensory body into the awareness of the highest Light vibrations.

*Open your eyes. Focus your senses outwards to the
candle flame. Commence the mantra breathing for
three in-breaths to reconnect your senses to Light.*

Draw the senses inwards by closing the eyes. Slowly
breathe light up through your nose to reach the internal
flame in your third eye chakra. Hold your breath in your
lungs as you focus the light from the third eye chakra upwards to exit through the crown chakra to seek and connect to the highest vibration of the Light of the universe.
As you slowly exhale, ask the highest Light to connect
and ignite your senses into the reality of the highest Light
vibrations.

*Open your eyes. Focus your senses outwards to the
candle flame. Commence the mantra breathing for
three in-breaths to reconnect your senses to Light.*

Draw the senses inwards by closing the eyes. Slowly breathe light up through your nose to reach the internal flame in your third eye chakra. Hold your breath
in your lungs as you focus the light from the third eye
chakra upwards to exit through the crown chakra to seek
and connect to the highest vibration of the Light of the
universe. As you slowly exhale, ask the highest Light to
awaken the Light in the solar plexus chakra to enable it
to connect to the highest Light vibration for support and
influence.

*Open your eyes. Focus your senses outwards to the
candle flame. Commence the mantra breathing for
three in-breaths to reconnect your senses to Light.*

Draw the senses inwards by closing the eyes. Slowly
breathe light up through your nose to reach the internal
flame in your third eye chakra. Hold your breath in your
lungs as you focus the light from the third eye chakra upwards to exit through the crown chakra to seek and connect to the highest vibration of the Light of the universe.
As you slowly exhale, ask the highest Light to ignite and
spin the solar plexus chakra existence into the intention
of the highest Light vibrations while realigning it to its
correct position in the centre top of the stomach.

*Open your eyes. Focus your senses outwards to the
candle flame. Commence the mantra breathing for
three in-breaths to reconnect your senses to Light.*

6. Sacral Chakra

Draw the senses inwards by closing the eyes. Slowly
breathe light up through your nose to reach the internal
flame in your third eye chakra. Hold your breath in your
lungs as you focus the light from the third eye chakra upwards to exit through the crown chakra to seek and connect to the highest vibration of the Light of the universe.
As you slowly exhale, ask the highest Light to awaken

your sensory body into the awareness of the highest Light vibrations.

Open your eyes. Focus your senses outwards to the candle flame. Commence the mantra breathing for three in-breaths to reconnect your senses to Light.

Draw the senses inwards by closing the eyes. Slowly breathe light up through your nose to reach the internal flame in your third eye chakra. Hold your breath in your lungs as you focus the light from the third eye chakra upwards to exit through the crown chakra to seek and connect to the highest vibration of the Light of the universe. As you slowly exhale, ask the highest Light to connect and ignite your senses into the reality of the highest Light vibrations.

Open your eyes. Focus your senses outwards to the candle flame. Commence the mantra breathing for three in-breaths to reconnect your senses to Light.

Draw the senses inwards by closing the eyes. Slowly breathe light up through your nose to reach the internal flame in your third eye chakra. Hold your breath in your lungs as you focus the light from the third eye chakra upwards to exit through the crown chakra to seek and connect to the highest vibration of the Light of the universe. As you slowly exhale, ask the highest Light to awaken the Light in the sacral chakra to enable it to connect to the highest Light vibration for support and influence.

Open your eyes. Focus your senses outwards to the candle flame. Commence the mantra breathing for three in-breaths to reconnect your senses to Light.

Draw the senses inwards by closing the eyes. Slowly breathe light up through your nose to reach the internal flame in your third eye chakra. Hold your breath in your lungs as you focus the light from the third eye chakra upwards to exit through the crown chakra to seek and connect to the highest vibration of the Light of the universe. As you slowly exhale, ask the highest Light to ignite and spin the sacral chakra existence into the intention of the highest Light vibrations while realigning it to its correct position in the centre of the belly just below the belly button.

Open your eyes. Focus your senses outwards to the candle flame. Commence the mantra breathing for three in-breaths to reconnect your senses to Light.

7. Base Chakra

Draw the senses inwards by closing the eyes. Slowly breathe light up through your nose to reach the internal flame in your third eye chakra. Hold your breath in your lungs as you focus the light from the third eye chakra

upwards to exit through the crown chakra to seek and connect to the highest vibration of the Light of the universe.
As you slowly exhale, ask the highest Light to awaken
your sensory body into the awareness of the highest Light
vibrations.

*Open your eyes. Focus your senses outwards to the
candle flame. Commence the mantra breathing for
three in-breaths to reconnect your senses to Light.*

Draw the senses inwards by closing the eyes. Slowly
breathe light up through your nose to reach the internal
flame in your third eye chakra. Hold your breath in your
lungs as you focus the light from the third eye chakra upwards to exit through the crown chakra to seek and connect to the highest vibration of the Light of the universe.
As you slowly exhale, ask the highest Light to connect
and ignite your senses into the reality of the highest Light
vibrations.

*Open your eyes. Focus your senses outwards to the
candle flame. Commence the mantra breathing for
three in-breaths to reconnect your senses to Light.*

Draw the senses inwards by closing the eyes. Slowly breathe light up through your nose to reach the internal flame in your third eye chakra. Hold your breath
in your lungs as you focus the light from the third eye
chakra upwards to exit through the crown chakra to seek

and connect to the highest vibration of the Light of the universe. As you slowly exhale, ask the highest Light to awaken the Light in the base chakra to enable it to connect to the highest Light vibration for support and influence.

Open your eyes. Focus your senses outwards to the candle flame. Commence the mantra breathing for three in-breaths to reconnect your senses to Light.

Draw the senses inwards by closing the eyes. Slowly breathe light up through your nose to reach the internal flame in your third eye chakra. Hold your breath in your lungs as you focus the light from the third eye chakra upwards to exit through the crown chakra to seek and connect to the highest vibration of the Light of the universe. As you slowly exhale, ask the highest Light to ignite and spin the base chakra existence into the intention of the highest Light vibrations while realigning it to its correct position in the base of the spine.

Open your eyes. Focus your senses outwards to the candle flame. Commence the mantra breathing for three in-breaths to reconnect your senses to Light.

8. & 9. Feet Chakras

Draw the senses inwards by closing the eyes. Slowly breathe light up through your nose to reach the internal

flame in your third eye chakra. Hold your breath in your lungs as you focus the light from the third eye chakra upwards to exit through the crown chakra to seek and connect to the highest vibration of the Light of the universe. As you slowly exhale, ask the highest Light to awaken your sensory body into the awareness of the highest Light vibrations.

Open your eyes. Focus your senses outwards to the candle flame. Commence the mantra breathing for three in-breaths to reconnect your senses to Light.

Draw the senses inwards by closing the eyes. Slowly breathe light up through your nose to reach the internal flame in your third eye chakra. Hold your breath in your lungs as you focus the light from the third eye chakra upwards to exit through the crown chakra to seek and connect to the highest vibration of the Light of the universe. As you slowly exhale, ask the highest Light to connect and ignite your senses into the reality of the highest Light vibrations.

Open your eyes. Focus your senses outwards to the candle flame. Commence the mantra breathing for three in-breaths to reconnect your senses to Light.

Draw the senses inwards by closing the eyes. Slowly breathe light up through your nose to reach the internal flame in your third eye chakra. Hold your breath in your lungs as you focus the light from the third eye chakra upwards to exit through the crown chakra to seek and connect to the highest vibration of the Light of the universe. As you slowly exhale, ask the highest Light to awaken the Light in the feet chakras to enable them to connect to the highest Light vibration for support and influence.

Open your eyes. Focus your senses outwards to the candle flame. Commence the mantra breathing for three in-breaths to reconnect your senses to Light.

Draw the senses inwards by closing the eyes. Slowly breathe light up through your nose to reach the internal flame in your third eye chakra. Hold your breath in your lungs as you focus the light from the third eye chakra upwards to exit through the crown chakra to seek and connect to the highest vibration of the Light of the universe. As you slowly exhale, ask the highest Light to ignite and spin the feet chakras into the reality of the highest Light vibrations while realigning them to their correct position in the sole of each foot.

Open your eyes. Focus your senses outwards to the candle flame. Commence the mantra breathing for three in-breaths to reconnect your senses to Light.

Close your eyes and refocus all the senses internally on the Light in the heart chakra and to your regular mantra breathing.

Remember, your chakras and senses are realigned and ignited into the brilliance of the highest Light vibrations.

Feel the vibrancy of Light within you.

Please sit as you continue with your mantra breathing.

Use your senses to interpret what you feel or sense from Light.

Remember, you are sitting in a sacred, protected space of Light.

Invite Light to help you to explore Light as you sit in the awareness of Light.

If unwelcome thoughts try to get your attention, detach from them by focusing on your mantra breathing.

After twenty in-breaths, or ten minutes which you can extend as you gain confidence in your meditating skills, draw your awareness back to the Light of the heart chakra and thank Light from the highest vibration for visiting you. It is essential to deliberately RELEASE this Light back upwards to the highest Light of the universe as you close your meditation.

Before you open your eyes and become physical again, it is essential to ground your aligned chakras and Light vibrations into your conscious everyday mindset.

Grounding

Begin by placing your hand on your head and imagining your hand is a beacon of bright shining Light. Imagine you are directing its Light downwards through the realigned internal chakra system. The Light enters the ground by exiting through the feet chakras, delving deep into the earth's energies to develop massive tree-like roots helping you to remain in a Light awareness until next time.

Insights that help build your Light Awareness

Potential Meditation Experiences

The experiences during this meditation are profound to you.

It would help if you were alert in your senses and detached from your mind to get a complete interpretation of the sensations you felt during this meditation.

In this meditation, do not seek the familiar learning of the mind or the comfort zones you took on as a child.

Challenge yourself to interpret the highest vibration of Light for your wisdom.

When you feel your senses vibrating in Light, please ask Light some questions.

For example:

What am I sensing?

Can I sense the energy in the room?

Please, Light, help me interpret my sensations, so I will know them in the future.

Accept the answers you interpret thoroughly.

Do not expect to receive instant answers, but they may manifest in future meditations.

If your mind is troublesome, revert to mantra breathing and sense the Light of the mantra.
To grow and evolve, you need to sense or feel Light.

Insights that help build your Light Awareness

There Is No Easy Way

There are no easy options when you begin your journey to finding Light.

There are no shortcuts.

There are no fast tracks.

You must want to connect to Light.

Your intention must be to connect to Light and not any other form of spiritual or religious invisibility.

Your intention must be to connect to your sensory Light body.

Your choice must be to feel the sensations of Light and accept them as your higher self.

It is vital to consciously build a boundary of Light discipline within your awareness of focus and intention.

Prayers for healing and Light Awareness

Please help me focus on my connection to Light by practising my mantra.

Light, please help me to accept that I am on a journey to finding myself at every level.

Light, please help me to feel courageous as I doubt what I am doing.

Light, please help me to sense Light.

Light, please help me see the difference between my bravado mind and my intention to connect to Light and give me the courage to change how I think.

Insights that help build your Light Awareness

Respect

P lease help me sense and accept the true meaning of respect.

First, I need to respect my Light awareness.

I need to respect my truth.

I need to respect my intuited thoughts and feelings.

I need to respect the sensations of Light I sense during my meditation.

I need to respect my pain.

I must respect others.

Prayers for healing and Light Awareness

Light, please help me to recognise when I automatically disrespect Light.

Please help me detach from that disrespect and urge me to refocus my senses on Light.

Light, please help me to recognise when I automatically disrespect myself.

Please help me detach from that disrespect and urge me to refocus my senses on the mantra breathing.

Light, please help me to recognise when I automatically disrespect other people.

Please help me detach from the learned disrespect and refocus my senses on the mantra breathing.

Insights that help build your Light Awareness

Observance

I pray for courage daily when I light my candle as I endeavour to live my life in Light awareness.

I pray for courage when I self-heal.

Light always gives me the strength to recognise the thoughts I need to change and release.

When I begin to change and release a thought, I focus on the thought initially by placing a candle flame between the thought in my bravado mind and my Light awareness.

The thought I need to detach from is a mental barrier I have created and put in place to protect the vulnerable me in my mind. When I find that learned thought, I tease it out until I can recognise when I learned it. Then, I release the learning barrier by changing the learned thought into an empowered thought of insight and Light. I find the emotions or feelings in the thought and cleanse them from my awareness, and I fill the area of my learning with the unconditional love of Light.

Sometimes there is more than one feeling in a thought.

It is vital to find each learned pained feeling, recognise the reason for the pain, and change the learning of pain into an awareness of unconditional love of Light.

There are no shortcuts to healing.

Insights that help build your Light Awareness

The Differences Between an Empowered Thought, a Positive Thought And a Powerful Thought

There is no pain, no learning in an empowering thought or viewpoint.

There is no memory contained in an empowered thought.

There is Light awareness.

In a positive thought, there is always a negative feeling that you need to suppress or deny.

In a powerful thought, there is always a want for power which suppresses the corresponding powerless feeling.

In a negative thought or feeling, there is pain.

Prayers for healing and Light Awareness

Please help me see that when I dwell on painful emotions or spin my automatic positive thoughts in my mind, I am not in Light awareness.

Please help me recognise when my automatic disempowered thoughts within my inner mind are automatically

146

influenced by the powerful messages constantly projected from the collective consciousness.

When I automatically regress to my learning, Light helps me refocus my senses back to Light by reminding me to do my mantra breathing.

Insights that help build your Light Awareness

Power

P ower is an illusion.

The search for power is a journey of tricks and fables.

There is no healing in the perception of power because the perception is fake.

Healing cannot happen through the power of the mind.

There is no power in Light.

There is the unconditional love of God.

There is your perspective of Light.

Light is reflective of a God that makes everything possible.

God enhances and supports all mindsets.

Insights that help build your Light Awareness

What is the duplicitous nature of the hierarchy of power?

The knowledgeable hierarchies within our societies tell ordinary people to believe we are all children in the eyes of God.

This statement is a lie as I now believe it is the purpose of each human being to evolve into their higher self, their Light within. People can only seek and connect to their higher self by taking full responsibility for their whole self. You can only take full responsibility for the entire self from an adult perspective.

Prayers for healing and Light Awareness

Please help me stand up from my knees in my inner mind and find the courage to seek and become myself, the Light within, my higher self.

Insights that help build your Light Awareness

An Inspired Thought

The following is an example of an inspired thought I knew I must not ignore.

I woke up asking myself, 'Have I spent too long writing? Should I stop?'

Instantly I began to look at my reasons for continuing to write.

Has writing become a habit, an excuse not to challenge me in different aspects of my work?

Am I using my writing as an avoidance mechanism to not share my healing awareness?

Is my automatic avoidance of the learned behaviour in my mind controlling my inspired writing?

I woke up hearing, "Stop; you must stop."

I accepted the thought and observed my mind concerning how to 'stop' my thoughts or behaviour. I observed my habit of not knowing how to 'stop' when to give up or to stop my thinking or behaviour. I give all of myself in my relationships until I reach a breaking point when anger or emotions take over my mind and relationships fail.

Prayers for healing and Light Awareness

Please, Light, help me see my automatic inner negative learning and thinking.

Please, Light, help me recognise my resistance and control and release these mechanisms from my mind.

Please, Light, help me to identify my lazy automatic thinking.

Please, Light, help me to recognise and challenge my automatic avoidance.

Insights that help build your Light Awareness

Fear

Why do I feel so frightened?
        Why can I not see my fear?
    What is frightening me?
    Why can't I see the pain that fuels my fears?
    When did fear become my inner reality?
    When did I become a frightened person?
    How can I break fear down into manageable fears that will not overwhelm me as I become aware?
    Fear is not love.

Prayers for healing and Light Awareness

Please, Light, help me to see my fears and not hide from them.

Please, Light, please give me the courage to recognise when my fears control me.

Please, Light, give me the insight to detach from each fear as I become conscious.

Please, Light, inspire me to understand that my higher self, the Light within, is not fear based.

Insights that help build your Light Awareness

My Fear

I remember when a friend told me I was frightened of my then-partner.

"Not at all," I smugly replied. "He loves me." I was on a ladies evening out at the time.

"Where will he be when you get home this evening?"

"Reading in bed," I replied.

"Does that threaten you in any way?" she asked.

"What do you mean?" I said to her, getting frustrated with the questioning.

"Will he question you about the evening?" she asked.

"Yes, I suppose but isn't that a normal conversation?" I replied. I silently reassured myself that I was not afraid of him.

A few weeks later, the following incident occurred in one of my readings with my mentor. He asked me if I was familiar with dependency. I replied that I thought so. He said, "You like to give the impression of being independent, but I see you as dependent and burdened. I get an image of two desks pushed together, the people sitting at them are facing each other. One desk is clear and unclut-tered, the other desk busy with papers and files."

I recognised the outline of the desks he described as our then-office.

I observed how I instantly justified my busyness by thinking I wasn't working hard enough; I noted that I must work harder. The reading continued as I heard him say I was taking on too much responsibility and working too hard.

I didn't know or understand at the time what he meant.

It was my fault if there was an unbalance in workloads.

I can recognise his words lodged within me, and it was to these insights that I defaulted afterwards when challenges between my partner and myself occurred. No-body ever told me I had worked too hard before in my life, or nobody ever told me I was a victim of my fear.

After the reading, I remembered some of my father's stories about how he faced his fear, and he would always finish a story by saying, face the fear. "Face it," he used to stress. I had no clue what he was talking about as a child or a young adult.

Where was this fear, I asked myself? Why was I not conscious of feeling frightened of my partner? I asked in meditation to reveal this fear to me.

Eventually, I found my relationship with my father. It was fear-stricken. I began to see that I had never chal-lenged him. I was mute in his company. I was childlike in my relationship with him.

I asked myself, in frustration, what has this to do with my relationship with my partner? I found my fear when I released my frustration and separated my emotions. I recognised the passive, pleasing relationship I learned from my parents, and within the family dynamic, I adapted automatically to the same learning in my relationship with my partner.

I was blind, I was deaf, and I was mute towards me, my inner self.

During these observations and conversations with myself, I revealed my mental barriers of control and ignorance, anger, resistance, denial and smugness.

Prayers for healing and Light Awareness

Light, please help me to recognise fear in my thoughts and emotions.

Light, please help me to recognise and release my resistance and help me to accept Light.

Please help me see that my unending resilience is causing pain in my mind and body.

Insights that help build your Light Awareness

My Senses

My senses permitted me to connect to Light and interpret Light.

I eventually accepted there are no limitations in Light's reality because Light freely shares its openness, wisdom and unconditional love with me.

I was free to explore any or all of these vibrations at will.

Eventually, I accepted that it was not other people or spirits blocking me – there were learned mental barriers spinning my bravado mind.

The barriers were the mental, emotional and spiritual blocks paralysing me in their pain and preventing me from advancing in my self-healing and expanding my Light awareness.

Prayers for healing and Light Awareness

Please help me to feel courageous in my Light awareness and not feel threatened by fear.

Insights that help reveal mental barriers

Chronic Pain

Nobody can lift chronic pain.
Nobody can stop anxiety.

These are states of mind created and influenced by your learned mental perspectives.

It is time to change how you think and feel.

If you make this change in your mind, you will change and alter your whole life.

Prayers for healing and Light Awareness

Please, Light, help me see my perception of weakness and release it.

Please, Light, help me accept the change that must occur within me.

Light, please inspire me to see and hear what I need to see and hear to help me begin healing.

Light, please help me to change my automatic default to my learning to an instant default of Light awareness.

Insights that help build your Light Awareness

There is Light

There is Light and Light awareness, there is Light consciousness, and there are boundaries of Light. Therefore, I must not engage my barriers of pleasing and false validation.

I must not please, and I must not seek validation or approval from other people.

I must always work through my boundary of detachment.

I must work from my awareness of compassion.

I will not be manipulated by myself and my thoughts or someone else's thoughts subconsciously, consciously or unconsciously. I found this sentence easy to write.

How difficult I find it to apply it to my mind?

My prayers and meditation provided the answers and healing for my pain.

I interpreted the Light within meditation to reveal and realign the chakras to their proper body positions, connected to Light and freely transmitting Light energies throughout the body.

The Light of the universe fully supports the Light within meditation.

The Light within meditation is the only way to begin healing and releasing the pain of the learned mind.

Insights that help build your Light Awareness

Emotions

Initially, emotions began their existence within the lost awareness of God's fragments as they fell from God's highest presence.

In their free fall into denser darker existences, they began to accept the different sensations they felt in the darkness as their identities. They accepted these sensations as their feelings that turned into unexpressed feelings that accumulated into what we call our emotions. The emotions became their automatic consciousness as their higher awareness of God faded. Darkness became their new reality, their new existence.

This journey reflects the emotional journey of each human being.

Prayers for healing and Light Awareness

Please, Light, inspire me to understand why professional people automatically spin me to reconnect me to my damaged, traumatised perspective.

Please, Light, help me feel compassion for those who dismiss me because they deem me weak and not strong.

Please, Light, inspire me to detach from my emotions and transmute them to Light during my meditations.

Insights that help build your Light Awareness

Light Experience

The Light within meditation is not just an experience of peace and harmony; it reveals the reasons for disharmony and unhappiness within the mind's conflicts, which reflect how we connect in all relationships.

Chronic pain, anxiety, and irrational thoughts are reasons pain and disharmony are unique to your mind's existence.

You may know some of these thoughts, but most remain hidden from your mind's perspective. They only manifest at a time of mental or emotional challenges or crises.

Please do not wait for the challenges or crises to arise to release these pain-filled barriers.

Begin the reveal and the release of them when you meditate on the Light within meditation.

Prayers for healing and Light Awareness

Please, Light, share with me the courage to accept the reasons for the disharmony in my mind.

Please, Light, shine your rays on my mental and physical pathway as I endeavour to follow your direction.

Please, Light, help me feel serenity to see where I need to self-heal.

Light, please help me achieve perseverance in my intention to help me to understand and clarify my self-healing.

The Third Meditation Add-On

The following paragraph is an add-on to the third meditation.

When you have practised this meditation regularly and are confident of the process, there is an add-on to the meditation, a new grounding exercise in Light that helps you feel fully connected and grounded to the Light within and connected to Light awareness.

When you have realigned all the chakras into a Light awareness during your meditation, open your eyes and focus all the senses outwards to the candle flame and commence mantra breathing for three in-breaths.

Draw the senses inwards by closing the eyes. Slowly breathe light up through your nose to reach the internal flame in your third eye chakra. Hold your breath in your lungs as you focus the light from the third eye chakra upwards to exit through the crown chakra to seek and connect to the highest vibration of the Light of the universe.

As you slowly exhale, ask the highest Light to connect with the following:

> ➢ the sensory Light in the crown chakra.
> ➢ to the sensory Light in the third eye chakra.

> to the sensory Light in the throat chakra.
> to the sensory Light in the heart chakra.
> to the sensory Light in the solar plexus chakra.
> to the sensory Light in the sacral chakra.
> to the sensory Light in the base chakra.
> to the sensory Light in the feet chakras.

As the highest Light connects to the sensory Light in the feet chakras, focus it on extending downwards from the feet chakras to connect with the earth's Light energy, which helps keep you in Light awareness and helps the healing process continue.

After your meditation, take some time to reflect on it and please write down the sensations you may have identified during your meditation.

The Fourth Meditation

The Release Of The Suppressed Energies Of The Mind And The Body

Releasing the suppressed energies of the physical and mental bodies back into Light existence facilitates healing and transmuting physical, mental, emotional, and spiritual pain.

> **WARNING:** *This meditation requires you to consciously feel your invisible chronic pain while releasing it from your mind and body. If you are fearful about feeling pain, do not attempt it.*

It is imperative that you are fully confident and trusting in the practice of your mantra meditation. It is equally important that you are fully competent in the realignment of the chakra meditation. Otherwise, you do not move on to this meditation.

Several release requests are listed after each chakra realignment which are potent healing desires. When this meditation is new to you, rather than trying to ask for all of the requests it is preferable to select which releases appeal to you from each chakra before you begin your meditation and ask these requests during your meditation.

You practice this meditation once a week, or if you prefer, you can practice one chakra at a time.

Sit on your chair and begin your journey of turning the senses inwards by gazing outwards at the candlelight.

All your breathing must inhale through the nose and exhale through the mouth.

Start this meditation by doing your mantra breathing for fifteen in-breaths.

As the mantra takes effect in your senses, you will feel the tension melting away from your body, permitting you to seek the Light within.

Open and focus the eyes and the senses on the
candle flame to reconnect to your Light breath.

Consciously slow down the breathing by counting to five as you breathe in, count to five as you hold your breath, and count to five as you exhale through the mouth.

Slowly breathe in Light for a count of five. Hold it in your lungs for a count of five. Breathe out Light for a count of five as you exhale through the mouth.

Slowly breathe in Light for a count of five. Hold it in your lungs for a count of five. Breathe out Light for a count of five as you exhale through the mouth.

Slowly breathe in Light for a count of five. Hold it in your lungs for a count of five. Breathe out Light for a count of five as you exhale through the mouth.

Slowly breathe in Light for a count of five. Hold it in your lungs for a count of five. Breathe out Light for a count of five as you exhale through the mouth.

Slowly breathe in Light for a count of five. Hold it in your lungs for a count of five. Breathe out Light for a count of five as you exhale through the mouth.

Close your eyes. Continue breathing in the rhythm of the mantra breathing.

Roll the eyes inwards towards the bridge of the nose area. You are looking for a reflected candle flame that may appear in your third eye space. With the eyes closed, continue to breathe, and say the mantra for three in-breaths.

Slowly breathe Light up through the nose to reach the internal flame in your third eye chakra. Hold your breath in your lungs. Focus the Light from the third eye chakra downwards to connect to the Light in the heart chakra. Slowly exhale Light through the mouth for a count of five.

Next, slowly breathe Light up through the nose to reach the internal flame in your third eye chakra. Hold your breath in your lungs. Focus the Light from the third eye chakra downwards to connect to the Light in the heart chakra. Slowly exhale Light through the mouth for a count of five.

Again, slowly breathe Light up through the nose to reach the internal flame in your third eye chakra. Hold your breath in your lungs. Focus the Light from the third eye chakra downwards to connect to the Light in the heart

chakra. Slowly exhale Light through the mouth for a count of five.

Let us begin our meditation.

1. Crown Chakra

Draw the senses inwards by closing the eyes. Slowly breathe light up through your nose to reach the internal flame in your third eye chakra. Hold your breath in your lungs as you focus the light from the third eye chakra upwards to exit through the crown chakra to seek and connect to the highest vibration of the Light of the universe. As you slowly exhale, ask the highest Light to awaken your sensory body into the awareness of the highest Light vibrations.

Open your eyes. Focus your senses outwards to the candle flame. Commence the mantra breathing for three in-breaths to reconnect your senses to Light.

Draw the senses inwards by closing the eyes. Slowly breathe light up through your nose to reach the internal flame in your third eye chakra. Hold your breath in your lungs as you focus the light from the third eye chakra upwards to exit through the crown chakra to seek and connect to the highest vibration of the Light of the universe. As you slowly exhale, ask the highest Light to connect and ignite your senses into the reality of the highest Light vibrations.

*Open your eyes. Focus your senses outwards to the
candle flame. Commence the mantra breathing for
three in-breaths to reconnect your senses to Light.*

Draw the senses inwards by closing the eyes. Slowly
breathe light up through your nose to reach the internal
flame in your third eye chakra. Hold your breath in your
lungs as you focus the light from the third eye chakra upwards to exit through the crown chakra to seek and connect to the highest vibration of the Light of the universe.
As you slowly exhale, ask the highest Light to awaken the
Light in the crown chakra to enable it to connect to the
highest Light vibration for support and influence.

*Open your eyes. Focus your senses outwards to the
candle flame. Commence the mantra breathing for
three in-breaths to reconnect your senses to Light.*

Draw the senses inwards by closing the eyes. Slowly
breathe light up through your nose to reach the internal
flame in your third eye chakra. Hold your breath in your
lungs as you focus the light from the third eye chakra upwards to exit through the crown chakra to seek and connect to the highest vibration of the Light of the universe.
As you slowly exhale, ask the highest Light to ignite and
spin the crown chakra existence into the intention of the
highest Light vibrations while realigning it to its correct
position on the top of the head.

*Open your eyes. Focus your senses outwards to the
candle flame. Commence the mantra breathing for
three in-breaths to reconnect your senses to Light.*

Please close your eyes and keep them closed.

On the next in-breath ask Light to align and ignite
the crown chakra into the brilliance of Light itself and to
extend this Light into every sensory and physical cell of
the brain and the brain function.

Exhale slowly.

On the next in-breath ask Light to release the dense,
imprinted, learned, painful constraints of religious teachings in this chakra.

Exhale slowly.

On the next in-breath ask Light to solidify the crown
chakra channel between the Light of the heart chakra
and the aura to the highest vibration of the Light of the
universe.

Exhale slowly.

On the next in-breath ask Light to help you see chronic hidden suffering that may be causing irrational fears
and emotions fuelled by the learning within this chakra.

Exhale slowly.

On the next in-breath ask Light to extend the Light
of the crown chakra outside the head to build a boundary
of Light around the top of the head to protect the crown
chakra channel to Light.

Open your eyes. Focus your senses outwards to the candle flame. Commence the mantra breathing for three in-breaths to reconnect your senses to Light.

2. Third Eye Chakra

Draw the senses inwards by closing the eyes. Slowly breathe light up through your nose to reach the internal flame in your third eye chakra. Hold your breath in your lungs as you focus the light from the third eye chakra upwards to exit through the crown chakra to seek and connect to the highest vibration of the Light of the universe. As you slowly exhale, ask the highest Light to awaken your sensory body into the awareness of the highest Light vibrations.

Open your eyes. Focus your senses outwards to the candle flame. Commence the mantra breathing for three in-breaths to reconnect your senses to Light.

Draw the senses inwards by closing the eyes. Slowly breathe light up through your nose to reach the internal flame in your third eye chakra. Hold your breath in your lungs as you focus the light from the third eye chakra upwards to exit through the crown chakra to seek and connect to the highest vibration of the Light of the universe. As you slowly exhale, ask the highest Light to connect and ignite your senses into the reality of the highest Light vibrations.

Open your eyes. Focus your senses outwards to the candle flame. Commence the mantra breathing for three in-breaths to reconnect your senses to Light.

Draw the senses inwards by closing the eyes. Slowly breathe light up through your nose to reach the internal flame in your third eye chakra. Hold your breath in your lungs as you focus the light from the third eye chakra upwards to exit through the crown chakra to seek and connect to the highest vibration of the Light of the universe. As you slowly exhale, ask the highest Light to awaken the Light in the third eye chakra to enable it to connect to the highest Light vibration for support and influence.

Open your eyes. Focus your senses outwards to the candle flame. Commence the mantra breathing for three in-breaths to reconnect your senses to Light.

Draw the senses inwards by closing the eyes. Slowly breathe light up through your nose to reach the internal flame in your third eye chakra. Hold your breath in your lungs as you focus the light from the third eye chakra upwards to exit through the crown chakra to seek and connect to the highest vibration of the Light of the universe. As you slowly exhale, ask the highest Light to ignite and spin the third eye chakra existence into the intention of the highest Light vibrations while realigning it to its correct position in the centre of the forehead.

Open your eyes. Focus your senses outwards to the
candle flame. Commence the mantra breathing for
three in-breaths to reconnect your senses to Light.

Please close your eyes and keep them closed.

On the next in-breath ask Light to realign and ignite the third eye chakra into the brilliance of Light itself and to extend this Light into every sensory and physical cell of the third eye chakra.

Exhale slowly.

On the next in-breath ask Light to release the 'seeing' senses from the dark unknown shadows of control held within the bravado mind.

Exhale slowly.

On the next in-breath ask Light to extend its Light into every sensory and physical cell of the brain tissue and to engage all the brain's different functions,

Exhale slowly.

On the next in-breath ask Light to reveal and lift the invisible mental shadows within this chakra that may be causing chronic fear, physical disease, chronic depression, chronic pain and discomfort in this area of the body.

Exhale slowly.

On the next in-breath ask Light to extend the Light of the third eye chakra outside the head to build a sensory boundary around the head to protect Light's presence within the third eye chakra.

Exhale slowly.

Open your eyes. Focus your senses outwards to the
candle flame. Commence the mantra breathing for
three in-breaths to reconnect your senses to Light.

3. Throat Chakra

Draw the senses inwards by closing the eyes. Slowly
breathe light up through your nose to reach the internal
flame in your third eye chakra. Hold your breath in your
lungs as you focus the light from the third eye chakra upwards to exit through the crown chakra to seek and connect to the highest vibration of the Light of the universe.
As you slowly exhale, ask the highest Light to awaken
your sensory body into the awareness of the highest Light
vibrations.

Open your eyes. Focus your senses outwards to the
candle flame. Commence the mantra breathing for
three in-breaths to reconnect your senses to Light.

Draw the senses inwards by closing the eyes. Slowly
breathe light up through your nose to reach the internal
flame in your third eye chakra. Hold your breath in your
lungs as you focus the light from the third eye chakra upwards to exit through the crown chakra to seek and connect to the highest vibration of the Light of the universe.
As you slowly exhale, ask the highest Light to connect
and ignite your senses into the reality of the highest Light
vibrations.

Open your eyes. Focus your senses outwards to the candle flame. Commence the mantra breathing for three in-breaths to reconnect your senses to Light.

Draw the senses inwards by closing the eyes. Slowly breathe light up through your nose to reach the internal flame in your third eye chakra. Hold your breath in your lungs as you focus the light from the third eye chakra upwards to exit through the crown chakra to seek and connect to the highest vibration of the Light of the universe. As you slowly exhale, ask the highest Light to awaken the Light in the throat chakra to enable it to connect to the highest Light vibration for support and influence.

Open your eyes. Focus your senses outwards to the candle flame. Commence the mantra breathing for three in-breaths to reconnect your senses to Light.

Draw the senses inwards by closing the eyes. Slowly breathe light up through your nose to reach the internal flame in your third eye chakra. Hold your breath in your lungs as you focus the light from the third eye chakra upwards to exit through the crown chakra to seek and connect to the highest vibration of the Light of the universe. As you slowly exhale, ask the highest Light to ignite and spin the throat chakra existence into the intention of the highest Light vibrations while realigning it to its correct position in the centre of the throat and neck.

Open your eyes. Focus your senses outwards to the candle flame. Commence the mantra breathing for three in-breaths to reconnect your senses to Light.

Please close your eyes and keep them closed.

On the next in-breath ask Light to ignite the throat chakra into the brilliance of Light itself and extend this Light into every sensory and physical cell of the throat chakra.

Exhale slowly

On the next in-breath ask Light to release the senses of taste, smell, hearing and voice from the control of the bravado mind.

Exhale slowly.

On the next in-breath ask Light to realign and ignite the different functions of the mouth and throat, the glands, the swallowing muscle, the taste buds, the tongue, the nerves, veins and the voice box into Light.

Exhale slowly.

On the next in-breath ask Light to realign and ignite the energies of the bone structure of the neck's vertebrae back to a Light reality.

Exhale slowly.

On the next in-breath ask Light to lift the invisible imprinted learned mental blocks from the throat and neck chakra that may be controlling your voice and causing chronic fears, fuelling chronic emotions, physical disease, and general discomfort in this area of the body.

Exhale slowly

On the next in-breath ask Light to extend the Light of the throat chakra outwards outside the neck and shoulders to build a sensory boundary of Light around the throat and neck to protect Light's presence within the throat chakra.

Exhale slowly.

Open your eyes. Focus your senses outwards to the candle flame. Commence the mantra breathing for three in-breaths to reconnect your senses to Light.

4. Heart Chakra

Draw the senses inwards by closing the eyes. Slowly breathe light up through your nose to reach the internal flame in your third eye chakra. Hold your breath in your lungs as you focus the light from the third eye chakra upwards to exit through the crown chakra to seek and connect to the highest vibration of the Light of the universe. As you slowly exhale, ask the highest Light to awaken your sensory body into the awareness of the highest Light vibrations.

Open your eyes. Focus your senses outwards to the candle flame. Commence the mantra breathing for three in-breaths to reconnect your senses to Light.

Draw the senses inwards by closing the eyes. Slowly breathe light up through your nose to reach the internal

flame in your third eye chakra. Hold your breath in your lungs as you focus the light from the third eye chakra upwards to exit through the crown chakra to seek and connect to the highest vibration of the Light of the universe. As you slowly exhale, ask the highest Light to connect and ignite your senses into the reality of the highest Light vibrations.

Open your eyes. Focus your senses outwards to the candle flame. Commence the mantra breathing for three in-breaths to reconnect your senses to Light.

Draw the senses inwards by closing the eyes. Slowly breathe light up through your nose to reach the internal flame in your third eye chakra. Hold your breath in your lungs as you focus the light from the third eye chakra upwards to exit through the crown chakra to seek and connect to the highest vibration of the Light of the universe. As you slowly exhale, ask the highest Light to awaken the Light in the heart chakra to enable it to connect to the highest Light vibration for support and influence.

Open your eyes. Focus your senses outwards to the candle flame. Commence the mantra breathing for three in-breaths to reconnect your senses to Light.

Draw the senses inwards by closing the eyes. Slowly breathe light up through your nose to reach the internal flame in your third eye chakra. Hold your breath in your

lungs as you focus the light from the third eye chakra upwards to exit through the crown chakra to seek and connect to the highest vibration of the Light of the universe. As you slowly exhale, ask the highest Light to ignite and spin the heart chakra existence into the intention of the highest Light vibrations while realigning it to its correct position in the centre of the chest in the breastbone.

Open your eyes. Focus your senses outwards to the candle flame. Commence the mantra breathing for three in-breaths to reconnect your senses to Light.

Draw the senses inwards by closing the eyes. Slowly breathe light up through your nose to reach the internal flame in your third eye chakra. Hold your breath in your lungs as you focus the light from the third eye chakra upwards to exit through the crown chakra to seek and connect to the highest vibration of the Light of the universe. As you slowly exhale, invite the highest Light to connect to the unique Light within the heart chakra to support and strengthen It whilst you meditate.

Open your eyes. Focus your senses outwards to the candle flame. Commence the mantra breathing for three in-breaths to reconnect your senses to Light.

As you gaze at the candle flame, welcome the Light from the highest vibration into your heart and ask for Its support as you meditate.

Please close your eyes and keep them closed.

On the next in-breath ask Light to ignite the heart chakra into the brilliance of Light itself and to extend this Light into every sensory and physical cell of the heart chakra.

Exhale slowly.

On the next in-breath ask Light to freely release the sensations of unconditional love so I can recognise how unconditional love feels.

Exhale slowly.

On the next in-breath ask Light to realign and ignite the energies of the physical heart, the lungs, the bone structure and the whole respiratory system to Light.

Exhale slowly.

On the next in-breath ask Light to lift the blocks of cognitive learning and knowledge from the chest area and the heart chakra that may be causing the invisible chronic pain, fuelling chronic fears, physical disease, emotional depression and discomfort.

Exhale slowly.

On the next in-breath ask Light to begin its invisible healing into the internal organs in the upper body functions.

Exhale slowly.

On the next in-breath ask Light to extend the Light of the heart chakra outside the chest area to build a sensory boundary of Light around the chest and back to protect Light's presence within the chest area.

Exhale slowly.

Open your eyes. Focus your senses outwards to the
candle flame. Commence the mantra breathing for
three in-breaths to reconnect your senses to Light.

5. Solar Plexus Chakra

Draw the senses inwards by closing the eyes. Slowly
breathe light up through your nose to reach the internal
flame in your third eye chakra. Hold your breath in your
lungs as you focus the light from the third eye chakra upwards to exit through the crown chakra to seek and connect to the highest vibration of the Light of the universe.
As you slowly exhale, ask the highest Light to awaken
your sensory body into the awareness of the highest Light
vibrations.

Open your eyes. Focus your senses outwards to the
candle flame. Commence the mantra breathing for
three in-breaths to reconnect your senses to Light.

Draw the senses inwards by closing the eyes. Slowly
breathe light up through your nose to reach the internal
flame in your third eye chakra. Hold your breath in your
lungs as you focus the light from the third eye chakra upwards to exit through the crown chakra to seek and connect to the highest vibration of the Light of the universe.
As you slowly exhale, ask the highest Light to connect

and ignite your senses into the reality of the highest Light vibrations.

Open your eyes. Focus your senses outwards to the candle flame. Commence the mantra breathing for three in-breaths to reconnect your senses to Light.

Draw the senses inwards by closing the eyes. Slowly breathe light up through your nose to reach the internal flame in your third eye chakra. Hold your breath in your lungs as you focus the light from the third eye chakra upwards to exit through the crown chakra to seek and connect to the highest vibration of the Light of the universe. As you slowly exhale, ask the highest Light to awaken the Light in the solar plexus chakra to enable it to connect to the highest Light vibration for support and influence.

Open your eyes. Focus your senses outwards to the candle flame. Commence the mantra breathing for three in-breaths to reconnect your senses to Light.

Draw the senses inwards by closing the eyes. Slowly breathe light up through your nose to reach the internal flame in your third eye chakra. Hold your breath in your lungs as you focus the light from the third eye chakra upwards to exit through the crown chakra to seek and connect to the highest vibration of the Light of the universe. As you slowly exhale, ask the highest Light to ignite and spin the solar plexus chakra existence into the intention of the highest Light vibrations while realigning it to its correct position in the centre top of the stomach.

Open your eyes. Focus your senses outwards to the candle flame. Commence the mantra breathing for three in-breaths to reconnect your senses to Light.

Please close your eyes and keep them closed.

On the next in-breath ask Light to ignite the solar plexus chakra into the brilliance of Light itself and to extend this Light into every sensory and physical cell of the solar plexus chakra.

Exhale slowly

On the next in-breath ask Light to extend its Light into all the digestive functions of the stomach and the whole digestion system.

Exhale slowly.

On the next in-breath ask Light to realign and restructure the system's physical energies, including the energies of the endocrine, the pancreas, the adrenal glands, the kidneys, the liver, and the upper colon, into Light awareness.

Exhale slowly.

On the next in-breath ask Light to realign and ignite the middle vertebrae energies to Light.

Exhale slowly.

On the next in-breath ask Light to lift the blocks of cognitive learning and knowledge that may be causing the invisible chronic pain, physical disease, depression, and discomfort in this part of the body.

Exhale slowly

On the next in-breath ask Light to extend the Light of the solar plexus chakra outside the stomach to build a boundary of Light around the waist area to protect the presence of Light within the solar plexus chakra.

Open your eyes. Focus your senses outwards to the candle flame. Commence the mantra breathing for three in-breaths to reconnect your senses to Light.

6. Sacral Chakra

Draw the senses inwards by closing the eyes. Slowly breathe light up through your nose to reach the internal flame in your third eye chakra. Hold your breath in your lungs as you focus the light from the third eye chakra upwards to exit through the crown chakra to seek and connect to the highest vibration of the Light of the universe. As you slowly exhale, ask the highest Light to awaken your sensory body into the awareness of the highest Light vibrations.

Open your eyes. Focus your senses outwards to the candle flame. Commence the mantra breathing for three in-breaths to reconnect your senses to Light.

Draw the senses inwards by closing the eyes. Slowly breathe light up through your nose to reach the internal flame in your third eye chakra. Hold your breath in your lungs as you focus the light from the third eye chakra upwards to exit through the crown chakra to seek and connect to the highest vibration of the Light of the universe. As you slowly exhale, ask the highest Light to connect and ignite your senses into the reality of the highest Light vibrations.

Open your eyes. Focus your senses outwards to the candle flame. Commence the mantra breathing for three in-breaths to reconnect your senses to Light.

Draw the senses inwards by closing the eyes. Slowly breathe light up through your nose to reach the internal flame in your third eye chakra. Hold your breath in your lungs as you focus the light from the third eye chakra upwards to exit through the crown chakra to seek and connect to the highest vibration of the Light of the universe. As you slowly exhale, ask the highest Light to awaken the Light in the sacral chakra to enable it to connect to the highest Light vibration for support and influence.

Open your eyes. Focus your senses outwards to the candle flame. Commence the mantra breathing for three in-breaths to reconnect your senses to Light.

Draw the senses inwards by closing the eyes. Slowly breathe light up through your nose to reach the internal flame in your third eye chakra. Hold your breath in your lungs as you focus the light from the third eye chakra upwards to exit through the crown chakra to seek and connect to the highest vibration of the Light of the universe. As you slowly exhale, ask the highest Light to ignite and spin the sacral chakra existence into the intention of the highest Light vibrations while realigning it to its correct position in the centre of the belly just below the belly button.

Open your eyes. Focus your senses outwards to the candle flame. Commence the mantra breathing for three in-breaths to reconnect your senses to Light.

Please close your eyes and keep them closed.

On the next in-breath ask Light to ignite the sacral chakra into the brilliance of Light itself and extend this Light into every sensory and physical cell of the sacral chakra.

Exhale slowly

On the next in-breath ask Light to extend into every function of the sacral chakra.

Exhale slowly.

On the next in-breath ask Light to realign and ignite the energies of the bone structure of the hips and the middle and lower spine to Light.

Exhale slowly.

On the next in-breath ask Light to realign and restructure the endocrine system's energies.

Exhale slowly.

On the next in-breath ask Light to lift the blocks of the learned and inherited cognitive and emotional constraints that may be causing invisible chronic pain, physical disease, depression, and discomfort in this part of the body.

On the next in-breath ask Light to extend the Light of the sacral chakra outside the body to build a boundary of Light around the lower waist at the top of the hips to protect Light's presence within the sacral chakra.

Exhale slowly.

Open your eyes. Focus your senses outwards to the candle flame. Commence the mantra breathing for three in-breaths to reconnect your senses to Light.

7. Base Chakra

Draw the senses inwards by closing the eyes. Slowly breathe light up through your nose to reach the internal flame in your third eye chakra. Hold your breath in your lungs as you focus the light from the third eye chakra upwards to exit through the crown chakra to seek and connect to the highest vibration of the Light of the universe. As you slowly exhale, ask the highest Light to awaken your sensory body into the awareness of the highest Light vibrations.

Open your eyes. Focus your senses outwards to the candle flame. Commence the mantra breathing for three in-breaths to reconnect your senses to Light.

Draw the senses inwards by closing the eyes. Slowly breathe light up through your nose to reach the internal flame in your third eye chakra. Hold your breath in your lungs as you focus the light from the third eye chakra upwards to exit through the crown chakra to seek and connect to the highest vibration of the Light of the universe. As you slowly exhale, ask the highest Light to connect and ignite your senses into the reality of the highest Light vibrations.

Open your eyes. Focus your senses outwards to the candle flame. Commence the mantra breathing for three in-breaths to reconnect your senses to Light.

Draw the senses inwards by closing the eyes. Slowly breathe light up through your nose to reach the internal flame in your third eye chakra. Hold your breath in your lungs as you focus the light from the third eye chakra upwards to exit through the crown chakra to seek and connect to the highest vibration of the Light of the universe. As you slowly exhale, ask the highest Light to awaken the Light in the base chakra to enable it to connect to the highest Light vibration for support and influence.

*Open your eyes. Focus your senses outwards to the
candle flame. Commence the mantra breathing for
three in-breaths to reconnect your senses to Light.*

Draw the senses inwards by closing the eyes. Slowly
breathe light up through your nose to reach the internal
flame in your third eye chakra. Hold your breath in your
lungs as you focus the light from the third eye chakra upwards to exit through the crown chakra to seek and connect to the highest vibration of the Light of the universe.
As you slowly exhale, ask the highest Light to ignite and
spin the base chakra existence into the intention of the
highest Light vibrations while realigning it to its correct
position in the base of the spine.

*Open your eyes. Focus your senses outwards to the
candle flame. Commence the mantra breathing for
three in-breaths to reconnect your senses to Light.*

Please close your eyes and keep them closed.
   On the next in-breath ask Light to ignite the base
chakra into the brilliance of Light itself and extend this
Light into every sensory and physical cell of the base
chakra.
   Exhale slowly
   On the next in-breath ask Light to extend into every
function of the base chakra.
   Exhale slowly.

On the next in-breath ask Light to realign and restructure this part of the body's physical energies of the base of the spine, the pelvic floor, and the bowel into Light awareness.

Exhale slowly.

On the next in-breath ask Light to realign and ignite the energies of the bone structure of the entire spine to Light awareness.

Exhale slowly.

On the next in-breath ask Light to lift blocks of the mental conditioning that are diminishing your self-worth, self-esteem and value as a person, which in turn causes invisible chronic pain, physical disease, depression, and discomfort in the body.

Exhale slowly.

On the next in-breath ask Light to extend the Light of the base chakra outside the lower body to build a boundary of Light around the lower hips at the bottom of the spine to protect Light's presence within the base chakra.

On the next in-breath ask Light to begin the invisible healing of the internal organs and their body functions.

Open your eyes. Focus your senses outwards to the candle flame. Commence the mantra breathing for three in-breaths to reconnect your senses to Light.

8. & 9. Feet Chakras

Draw the senses inwards by closing the eyes. Slowly breathe light up through your nose to reach the internal flame in your third eye chakra. Hold your breath in your lungs as you focus the light from the third eye chakra upwards to exit through the crown chakra to seek and connect to the highest vibration of the Light of the universe. As you slowly exhale, ask the highest Light to awaken your sensory body into the awareness of the highest Light vibrations.

Open your eyes. Focus your senses outwards to the candle flame. Commence the mantra breathing for three in-breaths to reconnect your senses to Light.

Draw the senses inwards by closing the eyes. Slowly breathe light up through your nose to reach the internal flame in your third eye chakra. Hold your breath in your lungs as you focus the light from the third eye chakra upwards to exit through the crown chakra to seek and connect to the highest vibration of the Light of the universe. As you slowly exhale, ask the highest Light to connect and ignite your senses into the reality of the highest Light vibrations.

Open your eyes. Focus your senses outwards to the candle flame. Commence the mantra breathing for three in-breaths to reconnect your senses to Light.

Draw the senses inwards by closing the eyes. Slowly breathe light up through your nose to reach the internal flame in your third eye chakra. Hold your breath in your lungs as you focus the light from the third eye chakra upwards to exit through the crown chakra to seek and connect to the highest vibration of the Light of the universe. As you slowly exhale, ask the highest Light to awaken the Light in the feet chakras to enable them to connect to the highest Light vibration for support and influence.

Open your eyes. Focus your senses outwards to the candle flame. Commence the mantra breathing for three in-breaths to reconnect your senses to Light.

Draw the senses inwards by closing the eyes. Slowly breathe light up through your nose to reach the internal flame in your third eye chakra. Hold your breath in your lungs as you focus the light from the third eye chakra upwards to exit through the crown chakra to seek and connect to the highest vibration of the Light of the universe. As you slowly exhale, ask the highest Light to ignite and spin the feet chakras into the reality of the highest Light vibrations while realigning them to their correct position in the sole of each foot.

Open your eyes. Focus your senses outwards to the candle flame. Commence the mantra breathing for three in-breaths to reconnect your senses to Light.

Please close your eyes and keep them closed.

On the next in-breath, ask Light to ignite the feet chakras into the brilliance of Light itself and to extend this Light into every sensory and physical cell of each foot.

Exhale slowly.

On the next in-breath, ask Light to extend its Light into every physical function of each foot.

Exhale slowly.

On the next in-breath, ask Light to extend its rays into the energies of every bone of each foot and ankle, healing and releasing the internal dysfunction of each foot and leg.

Consciously spread each foot as far as you can and flatten them into the ground.

Exhale slowly.

On the next in-breath, ask Light to lift the invisible collective and inherited learning and knowledge from the feet chakras that may be causing physical disease, physical unbalance, distress, depression, chronic pain and discomfort in the legs and feet.

Exhale slowly.

On the next in-breath, ask Light to reveal in its time the invisible obstacles that are permitting me to remain stuck in my mind.

Exhale slowly.

On the next in-breath, ask Light to extend outwards from the feet chakras to build a Light boundary around each foot to protect Light's presence within the feet chakras.

Please close your eyes and refocus your senses on the Light in the heart chakra by commencing your regular mantra breathing.

Please sit in the awareness of the brilliance of the highest Light.

Feel the vibrancy of your aura, your realigned chakras, and the vibrating Light from your physical body.

Invite Light to help you to explore Light as you sit in the awareness of Light.

Remember, you are sitting in a sacred, protected space of Light.

If unwelcome thoughts try to get your attention, detach from them by focusing on your mantra breathing.

Recognise doubt, fear and your need to feel secure and detach from them.

Ask Light for a single inspired thought into how you can physically help your self-healing journey.

After twenty in-breaths, or ten minutes which you can extend as you gain confidence in your meditating skills, draw your awareness back to the Light in the heart chakra and thank Light from the highest vibration for visiting you.

Thank Light for visiting you, and consciously release the highest Light to permit it to return home.

It is essential to deliberately RELEASE this Light back to the universe as you close your meditation.

Before you open your eyes and become physical again, it is essential to ground your newly aligned chakras and Light vibrations into your conscious everyday awareness by grounding yourself.

Grounding

Open your eyes and focus all the senses outwards to the candle flame and commence mantra breathing for three in-breaths.

Draw the senses inwards by closing the eyes. Slowly breathe light up through your nose to reach the internal flame in your third eye chakra. Hold your breath in your lungs as you focus the light from the third eye chakra upwards to exit through the crown chakra to seek and connect to the highest vibration of the Light of the universe.

As you slowly exhale, ask the highest Light to connect with the following:

- ➢ the sensory Light in the crown chakra.
- ➢ to the sensory Light in the third eye chakra.
- ➢ to the sensory Light in the throat chakra.
- ➢ to the sensory Light in the heart chakra.
- ➢ to the sensory Light in the solar plexus chakra.
- ➢ to the sensory Light in the sacral chakra.
- ➢ to the sensory Light in the base chakra.
- ➢ to the sensory Light in the feet chakras.

As the highest Light connects to the sensory Light in the feet chakras, focus It on extending downwards from the feet chakras to connect with the earth's Light energy, which helps keep you in Light awareness and helps the healing process continue.

After your meditation, take some time to reflect on it and please write down the sensations you may have identified during your meditation.

Also, please write down any thought patterns that may have kept repeating in your meditation.

Insights that help build your Light Awareness

Meditation Experiences

P lease help me feel courageous in my Light awareness and not feel inferior or threatened by the power of others.

Please help me to find acceptance that there are no quick fixes to healing the mind or the body.

I must remind myself that there is awareness of the self, Light, God, and the universe.

There are no drugs required to heal yourself. However, it would help if you had inner self-discipline to apply your boundaries of Light to protect your Light awareness.

Prayers for healing and Light Awareness

Light, please help me recognise my next steps to help me to evolve.

Insights that help build your Light Awareness

I Understand I Cannot Hide from Fear

I understand I cannot hide from fear. If I do, I will live my life through fear. The vibrations of fear are dark and forbidding forces of controlling energies. In fear, there is no Light, no insights, no inspiration, no balance, no responsibility, no boundaries, and no choices.

There is my ignorance which hides or denies my unknown hidden fears.

Insights that help build your Light Awareness

The Difference Between Auras

The single difference in each human being's aura is the vibration of Light the aura generates.

You are the only person who can find and attune to this Light, which is you and reflects you, your higher self.

How Do I Find The Automatic Invisible Barriers Of The Bravado Mind?

From a Light perspective:

Observe your thinking and responses to other people, and their responses to you.

Recognise your automatic responses and non-thinking, and you may see the mind-blocking mechanisms you use to protect yourself.

Observe the automatic habits and rituals in your mind that facilitate repressed and depressed thinking and feelings, and you will begin to understand your pain.

Recognise your mind dynamic, and you will see how you use your unique power by giving it automatically to people in your life.

Recognise how you fit into your family dynamic, and you will see how you shaped yourself all your life to fit and not be troublesome in your family, which has automatically extended to your adult relationships.

Recognise how you all interact with each other within your family dynamic, and you will see how you became the pleaser in your family by agreeing with the stronger personalities of your family by not telling your truth.

Recognise the inner mental conflict you interact with within your mind before you respond to people.

Recognise how your inherited religious teaching is influencing you in your current life. You will see how fear and pain that fuel your mind's perspective prevent you from looking to your higher self for guidance and direction.

Please begin to accept responsibility for ALL your feelings and emotions, and you will see how you project emotions outward toward other people and blame them for your pain.

Please accept responsibility for permitting other people to influence and control your feelings and emotions; you will see that you do not express your true feelings and emotions.

Please begin to take responsibility for your feelings by hearing and listening to your inner vibration, and you will sense the truth of your feelings, which is the voice of your higher self, your purest intuition.

Recognise the difference between how you feel and sense and what your thoughts tell you.

Accept responsibility for taking action to block people's projected dark emotions into your heart, and you will witness how the gift of detachment works for you.

Take responsibility for and accept and engage the act of detachment as the standard practice in your awareness which will permit you to accept your inspired, enlightened intuition.

Please welcome and accept Light influences into your heart and awareness and accept your responsibility for them.

I must remember I AM NOT MY LEARNED MIND and remember the following mantra:

> I am Light.
>
> I must take responsibility for my Light vibrations.
>
> I must be respectful of Light and my unique feelings.
>
> I must honour my Light.
>
> I must be conscious of applying my boundaries of Light to my Light awareness to stop the activation and powerful fluctuating of my learned mind.

In the following pages, I will list the words that thread together the automatically learned and suppressed mind that will reveal the learning, attitude and emotions impeding your individual growth in your awareness.

The words interlink to the mental barriers that form protective and controlling thoughts that isolate the inner mind in fear and pain.

Insights that help build your Light Awareness

Hate

People do not recognise hate as the poisonous darkness in their minds. Hate is usually masked and hidden within the mind by other more acceptable emotions of conditional love, judgement, control or self-righteous thoughts that allow us to blame the person we hate for our hating.

Hate is an automatically learned and vengeful emotion of 'conditional love' that spreads poison both in the hater and the hated. To hate automatically without questioning why you hate is treacherous to your self-confidence and self-esteem, affecting all your relationships.

Hate induces darkness; it is paralysing and can be incoherent, even illogical and possibly irrational in a person's mind.

Hate cultivates and nourishes feelings of anger and hostility automatically that influence people's minds in the same hate.

If you become aware of any of the following hate thoughts or emotions you hold towards anyone, please engage your detachment boundary instantly. Then, detach, using your Light boundary, from the negative words or emotions in your mind until you understand where their source began for you.

If your hate pushes you to violent thoughts or actions against someone, please immediately ask the authorities for professional help.

In your meditation, if one hateful feeling, a hateful thought, or a hateful action reveals in your Light awareness, instantly accept them as your mind. Then it is possible to begin your healing by deciding you no longer want to think, feel or behave in such a way again. The Light within, your higher self, will help you transmute this thought to Light vibrations, and you will feel unconditional love in your heart chakra as you begin to alter your thoughts to Light. Remember, the antidote to hate is to feel unconditional love.

Remember, if you refuse to let go of hate, you automatically subject your relationships and your children and their descendants to the darkness of this world's lower vibrations of pain and the influences of the darkness of the invisible spiritual world.

Prayers for healing and Light Awareness

Please, Light, help me to recognise hate in my thoughts, feelings or emotions.

Light, please help me not to hate.

Light, please help me to recognise my spiritual or religious hate.

Light, please help me to see hate.

Light, please help me to sense, feel and accept unconditional love.

Insights that help build your Light Awareness

My Learned Value

Most of us only understand the value of the pound we hold in our hands.

The value of value is learned from childhood and forms a huge mental block when you come to your growth and self-healing.

Through my Light awareness, I recognised that I never felt valued or validated during my whole life. I never knew I was not valued in honour, respect, truth, or unconditional love until I began my spiritual healing journey. Then, I recognised I did not honour or respect myself in truth or unconditional love. I only ever valued the pound I held in my hand.

I had no personal value at all in my inner self-awareness.

I had no validation of myself.

I had no idea how to value myself and my self-worth.

I still needed to learn how to validate myself.

I had no merit or worth in my awareness, feelings, or efforts to please people. I only recognised my value through how much money I had.

This thinking was revealed to me in a dream about eight years after my final divorce.

In my dream, I was working as a receptionist in a medical centre. I felt terrorised as I watched a man snatch my handbag from my desk. My credit and bank cards were in my stolen bag, and I recognised how distressed I was at the idea that I would have to tell my ex-husband about the theft. So, I was in a right flip of frustration and high anxiety when I physically woke up.

As I thought about the dream, I also thought I had healed the pain and hurt I revealed in my meditations from my divorce period.

When I wrote down my dream, I interpreted it as follows. First, I identified the medical clinic as my healing awareness and channel. I saw I was working as a receptionist, which meant I only worked superficially in my healing channel. So, I wasn't going further than the reception area to query the workings behind the scenes in my mind.

Secondly, I still found my worth and value through my connection to bank cards and my husband.

I had no creditworthiness within my learned mind.

I was not applying boundaries to my learned mind even though I was writing about boundaries and their importance in my healing.

From the dream, I understood that I needed to change a lot within my mind.

I needed to find a way of healing the deeper wounds and barriers in my mind that I was unaware existed within me.

I needed to find my husband's mental aspects in my mind, heal and release them.

I needed to cut ties with my husband.

I needed to begin consciously building the 'I' in my awareness and thinking.

I needed to change my perceptions of value and worth and draw my unique worth and value from my Light perspective.

I needed to apply my boundaries of Light, particularly detachment, to my learned mind.

I needed to detach from my husband and the automatic perspective that regressed my wants and fears to my marriage's comforts.

Insights that help build your Light Awareness

Manipulation

In my bravado automatic mind, I was so confident I was not a manipulating person. I assumed I was a truthful, honest person.

I assumed I understood manipulation, and in my automatic assumption, I thought I understood manipulation. My assumed thoughts denied me and prevented me from seeing a deeper manipulation that revealed my lack of personal awareness in my intention to love, honour and support my Light perspective. My self-healing insights revealed that I was manipulating, even in my healing channel. I assumed I was healing to the highest vibrations of Light, which was my intention. Then I recognised I was seeking validation for my healing in a very conditional way from this person who didn't know I was sending her the unconditional love of God. I recognised my automatic anger and irritation around this person. I brought this insight to my meditation hour and asked for help to sort it out. I saw I supported this person in jobs she asked me to do, but she never asked me for healing. I saw how I recognised her pain and automatically assumed she wanted to heal it. I put her on my healing list. I wanted to help her feel better and not be depressed. I was trying to heal her despite her determination to remain depressed. In my meditation, I realised she was a happy depressed person; she did not want to change herself and heal her pain. I was angry that she was not accepting my unconditional love of Light. I accepted that I needed to stop being with this person. I needed to heal my anger. I needed to see my conditions around my healing when there should be none.

I began to heal after I stopped looking outwards toward other people and the spirit's existence to tell me how to heal.

Prayers for healing and Light Awareness

Light, please help me to default my perspective to my Light awareness.

Light, please help me to see manipulation. If I can see manipulation in others, I will find self-manipulation within my mind.

Light, please help me to recognise the dismissive thoughts and feelings I have about people.

Light, please help me to recognise when I automatically dismiss my intuition and my insights.

Insights that help build your Light Awareness

My Learned Humility

From my bravado mind perspective, I was confident in my religious mindset and my learned humility.

The humility I learned from my religion was like a drug within me. It fed my senses and mind in continuous unknown darkness and invisible pain.

This religious drug automatically created a victim perspective, leaving me the victim, constantly feeling on edge in my inner mind. This edginess eventually revealed itself during meditation when I saw an image of myself on my knees looking upwards to seek recognition from a much holier and greater God.

From my knees posture, I saw my fearful perspective curled up in a ball, terrified of life, frightened of spirit, terrified of shadows, terrified of change, scared to talk, terrified of the darkness, terrified of failing.

I recognised that my religious and moral perspectives corresponded with and reflected my victim's existence in my inner mind.

My religious teachings infused false confidence of security because I assumed I knew the true God, the one God. Knowing my God was righteous made me feel superior because I loved Him, and he loved me, which protected me.

My pulpit perspective was revealed to my Light awareness when I began to see how I related my catholic opinion as I imitated and vocalised what the priests said without questioning their teachings. The priest is right; I often heard myself say to people who asked me for help.

I saw my unworthiness in my false humility as I called out to Jesus, the angels, the saints, and the mother of God to help me. I also saw when I refused to, or could not look or accept, the reasons for my invisible pain, which fed into my inherited passivity, so I could not stand up to help myself.

Prayers for healing and Light Awareness

Please, Light, help me see and hear my damaged self in my thoughts, actions and behaviour.

Please help me stand firm in my awareness of Light as I practice not pleasing other people. I must not seek validation or approval from others.

Please urge me to remember to work through my detachment boundary of Light. I must detach from pride.

Please urge me to remember that I must work through the compassion and empathy of my heart chakra.

Please, Light, give me the strength to not look outwards to the collective consciousness for power or knowledge. Instead, I must feel the value of the unconditional love of my inspirations of Light and honour my higher self, the Light within.

Insights that help build your Light Awareness

My Anger

I discovered my bravado learned mind was anger-based which influenced every thought and feeling in my mind. Therefore, I had many layers of anger to recognise and heal.

People mainly recognise anger from the emotional rages they see in action in other people's lives. Rarely do people associate anger coming from within their minds.

People live in a continuous rant of unexpressed anger and do not understand or admit they are angry or have substantial anger issues.

Some people think anger is strength.

Some people think anger is love.

Some people accept anger as powerful.

Some people accept anger as a standard way of speaking.

Some people think anger is clever because the rants sometimes contain truth.

Sometimes people think anger is protection from others.

Anger and frustration are very closely linked.

Anger hides in the intolerance, the unfulfilled, and the disappointed and dissatisfied emotions of frustration.

You need to understand that if you live with anger and accept it within your mindset as typical behaviour from others, you instantaneously make adjustments within your core self to accept and facilitate rage or anger. Accepting other people's anger as your everyday thinking means killing off a significant slice of your heart, your core self. You may accept other people's anger to ensure you live a peaceful life, but there is no peace in rage.

There is no love in anger.

Meditation will help you to recognise your suppressed automatic anger.

Prayers for healing and Light Awareness

Please inspire me to recognise my suppressed anger in my thoughts and responses.

Light, please inspire me with your influences of courage to help me find the courage to stand and face my anger in all its disguises.

I cannot recognise anger in my thoughts or my behaviour.

Please, Light, help me clear my frustrations so I can acknowledge my anger.

Insights that help build your Light Awareness

Compromise

Compromise is a learned coping mechanism by the bravado mind that mainly benefits the controllers and manipulators in your life.

Most relationships cannot survive without the input of compromise.

It is something automatically accepted rather than wanted in a relationship.

Unfortunately, people compromise automatically, and it balances in favour of the demanding wilful person who refuses to compromise in a relationship but demands compromise from other people. The middle ground of natural balance corrupts. The relationship begins to be undermined or devalued by the compromiser in the relationship. The compromised person makes too many concessions, leading to confrontation, frustration, anger, abuse, and belittling behaviour within the relationship. It triggers mental traits of pleasing, comforting, silence, and soothing in the compromised person.

A person must seek the truth of their relationship and its compromises and accept the resulting feelings and emotions before healing begins.

Prayers for healing and Light Awareness

Light, please help me to recognise compromise.

Light, please help me to understand compromise.

Please, Light, help me not to be intimated by the demands of compromise.

Insights that help build your Light Awareness

Control

The controlling mindset is a narrow perspective of the learned mind based on the influences of conditional love that constantly strives for power. Conditional love generates the automatic adherence to the hierarchy of society which feeds the automatic acceptance of mental and physical suffering that becomes normal within the collective mindset of society.

The family dynamic of thinking is reflective the society's collective mindset. The family dynamic of thinking and survival generates automatic control and power within the family dynamic of rule and manipulation, influence and oppression, loyalty and duty, and passivity and silence. Because this thinking is standard in the family dynamic, it becomes expected in the individual mind. Therefore, if you need to find control within your mind, you must recognise the limitation and restrictions somebody has over your free will, voice, thoughts, and feelings.

Prayers for healing and Light Awareness

Light, please help me to identify control within my thoughts.

Please help me sense Light so that I can recognise controlling thoughts.

Insights that help build your Light Awareness

Lies

To tell a lie is to say something that is not true, that is false. A lie by a liar is a conscious, deliberate effort to deceive and give a false impression about yourself or another person.

Deliberately telling a lie about a person is a violating method of destroying another person's truth and character.

It is abusive and disrespectful towards someone unaware of your lies and manipulation. Lying is blatant disrespect towards the person you are lying to, the person you lie about, and especially yourself.

Prayers for healing and Light Awareness

Light, please help me to recognise when I lie.

Light, please help me to know the difference between truth and untruth.

Light, please help me to express my truth.

Insights that help build your Light Awareness

Betrayal

B etrayal is another secret, invisible crime against the heart of a person you love or who loves you in return and who is unaware of your intention to hurt or damage them. If someone you love has betrayed you, it feels treacherous, almost an unbearable pain that feels like a knife in your heart.

If you betray someone you love, you also betray the core of yourself.

Betrayal is an actual treacherous crime against humanity and God.

Prayers for healing and Light Awareness

Light, please help me not hold on to pain.

Light, please help me to heal my heart.

Insights that help build your Light Awareness

Resilience

R esilience is an automatic barrier of protection within the bravado mind. It enables people to force themselves onward and forward in their mindset to recover too quickly from physical or mental setbacks. Or it can mean the mental flexibility to bend or be bent repeatedly without recognising physical or mental pain in the body.

This barrier can resemble a weapon used against the self when you keep pushing yourself up that invisible mountain without understanding the cost to yourself of your denial. You are hurting yourself when you suppress your feelings of pain and deny your intuition urging you to speak up and not to be silent or subservient to other people's opinions.

Prayers for healing and Light Awareness

Please, Light, help me recognise my automatic silence as a mental barrier to myself.

Light, please help me to voice my truth.

Insights that help build your Light Awareness

Dominance

D ominance is the ultimate tyranny of a powerful mindset.

The command wielded by the mind perspective of a dominant person is supreme.

There is no mercy; there is no other way.

The dominant mindset operates in powerful ignorance and arrogance and believes entirely in their ego, their 'right' way and alienates or destroys those mindsets who disagree.

Prayers for healing and Light Awareness

Light, please help me to recognise when others overpower me.

Light, please help me to voice my truth and my strength.

Please help me recognise if I have become a dominant person unknowingly in my mind.

Insights that help build your Light Awareness

Anger

Anger is a fire-filled emotion that simmers in the frustrations that build within the mind and erupts when you lose control. Anger builds from the violation of mental and physical abuse that reveals violent hurt, grievance and injury, annoyance and irritation, and fury or rage or a feeling of powerlessness fuelled over time by learned anger.

Frustration, resentment, and resistance are supporting emotions that keep you shackled in your anger.

Anger fuels many emotions within your mind, and it is best to begin to recognise one angry thought and detach from it in your meditation.

Prayers for healing and Light Awareness

Please, Light, help me recognise one angry thought or emotion at a time.

Light, please help me find the courage to stand and face my anger.

Insights that help build your Light Awareness

Self-Discipline

I deally, a person should learn self-discipline from parents and teachers. Unfortunately, children learn the pain of discipline through punishment and the control of adults. Children learn obedience and disobedience, chastisement and persuasion, strictness and control and pain that deplete confidence and self-esteem.

I direct people to understand the essential need for inner discipline in their inner minds and awareness in my meditation sessions.

I inform them that they must exercise their free will and choose to gain their unique awareness. It involves them being internally disciplined in their inner awareness to detach from their learned minds and pain. And to absorb what Light is sharing with them.

Inner discipline is necessary to advance in meditation and self-healing.

Prayers for healing and Light Awareness

Please, Light, help me not feel overpowered by insight and my need to heal to change my mind.

Insights that help build your Light Awareness

Entitlement

Entitlement is the automatically learned silence of privilege by the bravado mind, which is deadly in its destructive and painful behaviour towards other people.

Some people think entitlement involves their civil rights.

I think it is an automatically privileged superior mindset that demands its entitlement or a right to a person, power or property that does not belong to the entitled mindset.

It is also an automatic claim by the bravado perspective on relationships, which allows the entitled person to be disrespectful and unloving.

It is an automatic stance to a perceived place in the family's hierarchy and the collective society.

Entitlement fuels the automatic inbred greed and foulness of disrespect in a person's mind.

Prayers for healing and Light Awareness

Light, please help me to check my wants and desires.

Please help me to differentiate between my actual needs and my entitled wants.

Insights that help build your Light Awareness

Duty

Duty is an automatically learned secret unspoken obligation within the mind towards other people or society.

Duty learned from a very young age is tied up and confused with the cruel obligations of conditional love.

I have revealed that duty from a child's learned perspective supports an equally immature understanding of personal responsibility, which clouds what duty means. From this perspective, duty grows into a tremendous sense of burdened responsibility and isolated loneliness.

Learned duty and loyalty are very closely linked and go hand in glove with the learned family dynamic of thinking.

Duty and loyalty can fuel emotions of devotion, attachment or fear, anger and inferiority.

Prayers for healing and Light Awareness

Light, please help me to recognise duty in my thoughts.

Light, please help me to recognise loyalty in my thoughts.

Please help me feel responsible for my whole mind, to see and differentiate other people's mindsets and not be controlled by them.

Insights that help build your Light Awareness

Loyalty

"In general, loyalty is devotion and faithfulness to a nation, cause, philosophy, country, group, or person. However, philosophers disagree on the subject, as some argue that loyalty is strictly interpersonal and only another human being can be the object of loyalty."

Oxford Dictionary

I discovered that my learned sense of loyalty was a formidable obstacle that tied me into unbalanced relationships. I found it in my inability to voice an opinion because I feared being disloyal. I didn't speak to people because I was loyal to those who broke up relationships. Loyalty prevented me from finding and accepting the adult in my thoughts.

Since self-healing, I now use respect as a guidance tool in my relationship and with myself.

If there is no respect, then there is no relationship.

Insights that help build your Awareness

Guilt

The mother/daughter relationship is a typical mental block based on guilt learned automatically in the child's mind.

The process of self-healing begins with your intention to want to heal your pain.

Pain isn't always a physical open bleeding wound that we can see. More often, pain transmits through thought or feeling.

Your Light awareness will reveal the relevant patterns of the mind that maintain the invisible pain.

As you meditate, Light reveals a single opinion, a thought pattern, a memory, or an emotion you can identify and begin to recognise as pain that needs to be released.

When you recognise a thought, it is essential to begin detaching from it. Detachment is a crucial tool in self-healing as it enables you to stop fuelling your mind from the energies of the family mind dynamic.

For example, a duty thought comes into your mind during meditation in the shape of

"I have to phone my mother this evening like I do every other evening, even though I am visiting her at the weekend."

This thought can easily be dismissed as a 'reminder' to make the call without you considering that it may need healing.

Accept the thought and detach from it.

When you finish your meditation, write down the sentence. Each time you become conscious of this thought, detach from it. Continue to detach from it. Continue to observe it from a Light perspective. Soon the feelings and emotions underlying this sentence will come to the fore.

The first insight is the feelings of compulsion in that you have to call your mother, which may reveal the automatic childlike duty you feel towards your mother.

Are you frightened of your mother? Are you afraid not to call your mother? Does your mother upset easily and is prone to tears?

Duty is a heavy burden you learn from very early years, and it can keep you in a child mindset in the relationship with your mother. Yet, she is the adult –you remain the child, indebted, almost accountable to her in your mind.

You may also feel you have no choice in your relationship with your mother. Therefore, you must be obedient and comply with your mother's opinions and even her unsaid wishes.

Compliance is another learned behaviour from your child's years; it can also keep you in your child's learning. For example, you learned complete dependency on your mother. You learned total obedience, and as a grown adult, you still automatically obey her and depend on her for her thoughts and feelings.

As you begin your detachment from her, you must ask yourself, "Am I resentful of the time I have to give to my mother?" But, again, resentment is a learned thought process that can automatically spin you into the hidden emotions you are unaware of within your mind. The silent, automatic resentment you feel within yourself towards others in your immediate circle of friends and your relationships can reflect this resentment.

There are no instant answers to these questions.

These three insights about this sentence reveal your need to re-evaluate your relationship with your mother and how you are automatically copying or imitating your mother's ways as your way in your mind.

This work is very subtle, and it can be easily missed if you are not intentionally seeking healing.

When you have worked out the sentence's relevance, I recommend you immediately apply a detachment boundary of Light between you and your mother. Then, re-evaluate your feelings towards your mother – are you still childlike in your relationship with her? Do I address her in a child's way even though I am the adult? Do I love her conditionally? Does your love feel entitled?

Attune to your Light perspective when you begin your communication with her from an adult perspective, from your awareness of unconditional love. It is crucial you understand that you must be respectful towards her from this perspective, or this action can be exceedingly hurtful for you both.

From your Light awareness perspective, the following is an attempt to challenge yourself to be an adult by addressing her as an adult. "I hear you, Mother, and I understand. I love you, Mother, but I can only phone you at lunch hour from now as I have other relationships in the evening to keep and nurture, I am visiting this weekend, and we can catch up fully then."

When you begin the process of self-healing, it is essential to write down all your thoughts and actions.

Prayers for healing and Light Awareness

Light, please help me have patience with my impatient learned mind. It is important not to deny, suppress, or resist insights into my healing journey.

What Defines an Effective, Empowered Healer?

I experienced the raw, painful emotions projected by my teachers in particular and other people who delivered their knowledge of me from their pained perspectives. Their pained perspectives triggered and fuelled pain in my mind, making it impossible for them to teach, inspire, influence or lead me in any way except in pain, inferiority and inadequacy.

When I was a healer endeavouring to advance my spiritual healing career, the hierarchy cited my mental inadequacy in not being a suitable tutor. I understood then that they were looking for excellence in their tutors, ensuring the communication of knowledge learned from a college or university. However, as I reeled mentally from their rejection, it became evident that they were not seeking my higher self-perspective. So, I committed myself and my intention to become an evolved person based on the wisdom I interpret from Light. I interpreted Light's wisdom as my Light awareness, my wisdom with clarity and pureness of communication. If I shed my learned mental imprints and limitations, I could one day be an enlightened, aware person who could inspire others to heal themselves from their higher perspective.

My journey to becoming an enlightened, fully aware person in all aspects of who I am has become a life journey for me and is more important than life itself.

At the time, I was looking to become a tutor; I needed more insight into what was required to become this tutor. I thought or assumed I knew a lot about spiritual healing, but in hindsight, I knew little about healing and less about self-healing.

I needed to accept myself as someone who still hurts and feels pain because my heart chakra is now open as I work from a Light perspective. This means that people who judge me as weak and need to tell me their poisoned opinions about becoming stronger in their reflection. Worse still, they slap me down in anger because they think they are stronger than me and feel entitled to discard me.

Being an interactive human is workable because I interact through boundaries that protect me. Still, sometimes my boundaries are violated so harshly that I can die within myself from inflicted pain for days.

My experiences of being human and a communicator of excellence determine who I am in my consciousness, a person whose mind reflects Light's wisdom.

What are Past Lives?

From the beginning of evolution, imprints of humanity's history are automatically invisibly imprinted and carried in the individual mind, eventually revealing themselves as spiritual, mental and emotional pain.

The behaviour of past civilisation's actions and reactions, their dominance, brutality, cruelty, ignorance arrogance, punishments tortures, enslavement, famines, fears, wars, failures, betrayals, and their darkness are all hidden, buried, and suppressed in the individual mind of today.

These different imprints of previous civilisations are fundamentally the invisible, unknown prompters and influencers that drive the mind's perspective deeper into the learned automatic survival thinking for answers that fuels our irrational dark thoughts.

If today's humanity does not recognise these influences in their minds, they will fail to heal or transmute them in their thoughts and emotions. Consequently, I do not doubt that the future humanity will repeat the ferocious crimes and cruelties against fellow humans written and recorded very clearly in our history books.

Thus, each person needs to understand their mind and its vibration fully. The only way I know how to become fully conscious is to work from a Light perspective and through the boundary of detachment that allows you to observe thought patterns, thoughts, emotions, feelings and the internal spiritual influences that crucify people in invisible pain. Most of our hidden, unknown, invisible pain is related to the suffering existences of past lives because they automatically attach themselves to similar pain vibrations in people's minds. In addition, their memories, emotions, and spirits influence us unknowingly in our need to survive, which also drives the same mind into more darkness of pain.

From conception to experiencing delivery and the birth journey, I understand that our early learning and development are all sensations, feelings, and learning which are influenced heavily by the karma that aligns with the vibrations of past lives in the minds of the family dynamic.

A past life identity exists in the spiritual reality of the collective consciousness within the family dynamic. Spiritual identity is an image of a person that lived during previous life existences but, for some reason, did not evolve into higher vibrations when it passed from their physical life.

This spirit identity finds its comfort by nestling and attaching to a living person's mindset of similar pain vibration. Only when a person lifts the vibration of their mindset does it become possible to help this spirit identity evolve. This healing happens during a healing session or when a person becomes aware of them during meditation.

Many books and therapies explore past lives and why they influence our current lives.

Self-healing is the only way to empower and realign these spirit identities into self-awareness based on unconditional love without historical influences. If I become aware of irrational thoughts, I repeat the following prayer to help me detach from my irrational thoughts.

There is Light, there is Light consciousness, and there are boundaries of Light. I must not engage my learned mental barriers of pleasing and false validation.

I must not please, and I must not seek validation or approval from other people.

I must work through a compassionate boundary.

I will not be manipulated by myself and my thoughts or someone else's thoughts subconsciously, consciously or unconsciously. I refuse to allow invisible spirits and their emotions or irrational thoughts to drive me onward in my mind.

Absent Healing

I have spent about thirty years interpreting, understanding and accepting how Light and healing work.

I had to heal my mind and recognise my powerful learned ways of surviving before I became aware of my higher self, the Light within.

I had to see how I was spreading darkness and pain in the automatically entitled bravado mindset of my learned healing. I had to see how I approached my absent healing technique as casual and disrespectful.

I had to see my automatically entitled way when I expected God to do my absent healing. I had to see my disrespect for God as I robotically verbalised my requests for absent healing.

I had to see that I did not accept responsibility for my absent healing by automatically thinking, 'God knows what I mean.'

My absent healing technique is a unique channel of Light awareness that combines personal responsibility and respect for Light, my healing channel and the person receiving healing. During my absent healing, I share Light freely and unconditionally, but when I list a person's name for recovery, there is a direct Light connection with the person and Light. I am accountable and responsible to God for my absent healing as I am in all my work.

The following is an example of how absent healing sometimes works.

2016

I went to do a home healing visit with two elderly sisters. One was in the hospital for tests. So, I began my healing session with the sister who was home. Just as I was finishing her healing, the other sister came in from her hospital visit and instantly said to me, are you practising being in two places at once?

I said no and asked her what she meant.

She then said she just spoke to me in the hospital room, where she had some tests done.

How do I Practice Absent Healing?

At the end of meditation and before releasing the Light from the highest vibration, I consciously open all of my senses outwards by opening my heart chakra, similarly to how I open a door.

The Light in the heart chakra flows in abundance from the highest vibrations. I consciously direct this Light to the people on the healing list, to the Light in their heart chakras for healing. Also, share it outward to the world situations requiring conscious Light support.

When I complete this intention of sharing Light, I close my heart chakra as I would close a door. Then, I thank Light for working with me, and I release the Light back to its higher vibrations in the universe.

I consciously ground myself in my Light awareness.

If you elect to work with Light, always show your appreciation of the abundance of Light by thanking Light and God for your experiences of Light.

Please Review and Spread the Word

If you enjoyed this book, I would really appreciate if you could spread the word or leave a review on Amazon or Goodreads. Your opinion counts and it does influence buyer decision on whether to purchase the book or not. Thank you!

Lucy

Printed in Great Britain
by Amazon

27396262R00145